ARE WE LEADING?

KAUSHIK MAHAPATRA

INDIA • SINGAPORE • MALAYSIA

Notion Press

Old No. 38, New No. 6
McNichols Road, Chetpet
Chennai - 600 031

First Published by Notion Press 2020
Copyright © Kaushik Mahapatra 2020
All Rights Reserved.

ISBN 978-1-64783-528-6

This book has been published with all efforts taken to make the material error-free after the consent of the author. However, the author and the publisher do not assume and hereby disclaim any liability to any party for any loss, damage, or disruption caused by errors or omissions, whether such errors or omissions result from negligence, accident, or any other cause.

While every effort has been made to avoid any mistake or omission, this publication is being sold on the condition and understanding that neither the author nor the publishers or printers would be liable in any manner to any person by reason of any mistake or omission in this publication or for any action taken or omitted to be taken or advice rendered or accepted on the basis of this work. For any defect in printing or binding the publishers will be liable only to replace the defective copy by another copy of this work then available.

Contents

Acknowledgements   5

1. Are we leading?   7
2. The Leader in each one of us   11
3. What Leaders do   14
4. What's your Big why   20
5. Leadership Begins at home   26
6. Leadership at work   30
7. Are you leading by example?   40
8. Are you struggling right now?   44
9. Leading in tough times   48
10. Leading by your values   55
11. Leading with Ancient Wisdom   59
12. Emotional Intelligence for Leadership development   64
13. Empowering the young guns   68
14. Sharp minds – Mental health for future leaders   73
15. Don't just survive, thrive   77
16. Communicate with a difference   83
17. The path less travelled – Being Creative   91
18. Community leadership   95
19. Leadership development through sports   99
20. What schools don't teach   103
21. Parental Leadership   109
22. The futuristic teacher   120
23. Are there enough opportunities   130
24. Essential Soft skills for Leaders   135
25. Why do you need a coach or a mentor?   140
26. Leading a happy and meaningful life   145
27. Closure: It's all about a leadership mindset   153

Acknowledgements

The world needs better leaders more than ever. We live in an environment which is continuously changing. There are new threats almost every other day and hence a lot of scope for new opportunities and initiatives. There is still extreme poverty, hatred and lack of meaning in people and hence we need better leaders for peace, prosperity and purpose. We need leaders who lead themselves successfully before attempting to lead others.

The Book is dedicated to:

- to all the future leaders who are going to shape their own lives, their country and humanity in coming years.
- to my Mother and Father Sudeshna Mahapatra and Prabhas Mahapatra for being the greatest of the teachers and without whom this book would not have come into existence. Truly blessed to have you as my parents.
- to my Mother in law and father in law Shantilata Mishra and Nilambara Mishra for your constant guidance and always making me feel so special.
- to my wonderful wife Linki Mishra for her unconditional love and support despite my shortcomings. No greater light illuminates my path than the positive changes you have brought into my life.
- to my Children Rounak and Ronit for your profound love and caring. My children are my best role models.

Acknowledgements

- to my Loving sister and Brother Sobhna and Kausam for all those sweet childhood memories.
- to my teachers and mentors for always keeping the faith.
- to Indian Leadership Academy and thousands of colleagues, employees, executives, parents, youth, and teachers who has inspired and encouraged me to pen down my thoughts.
- to my Dear employees especially Ishani Mishra, Ankita Srivastava and Ruchika Garg for your suggestions and inputs on few important topics which helped me to complete this book. It is always a joy to work with you.
- to my friends and relatives for all the good advice, support and love.
- to my wonderful readers for picking up this book and giving your valuable time. Love you all.

1

Are we leading?

The last 22 years of my professional life has been a roller coaster ride. Being a trainer, coach, mentor, a parent, a corporate executive, a senior manager and a responsible global citizen I have had the privilege to connect with numerous people all over the world. What I could observe was, some of them had natural leadership qualities. They are incredibly successful and happy in both personal and professional lives.

Most people are leading a routine life and are busy to get their basic needs fulfilled. People who are into jobs are juggling between work and life with much difficulty and they don't seem to even think of what else they can do better in life. On the other hand, there are people who have wonderful ideas and motivation to create an impact in the society, but somehow fail to execute them.

Over the years, statistics say that only 1-3% of people really succeed. By success, I mean overall well-being and satisfaction in life. But this very tiny group of people also hint towards the possibility that others who aspire and work hard and finally do not get the desired results, are indeed missing something.

So, the million- dollar question is - What do these 1-3% people have that others don't?

Possible answers might be lack of vision, lack of action or other constraints which people find as strong and valid enough reasons for not being able to succeed.

An American author, George A. Sheehan once said "Success means having the courage, the determination, and the will to become the person you believe you were meant to be" and according to me it all begins with taking the first step and trying to work on it meticulously. And the very first step is to find out what you are meant to be.

Having met thousands of people from all walks of life, I have seen that most of them have shown the urge to change, to do something amazing, but sadly I never saw many of them sustain. The meaning that I make out of it is that with age, we all get hardwired and habitual, so it is very difficult to unlearn something and adapt quickly to a behavioral change. In short, creating a change in our thinking patterns is not easy, but isn't it required to do something new in life? I think it is not only required; it is in fact mandatory!

I only wish we all had an insight to our inherent leadership qualities and our true personality at an early age. We all would be so different, so productive then!

We need to really discover what exposure and opportunities can be given to children from now on, before their beliefs and personalities have solidified.

A keen observation is that we largely associate leadership with professional adults who are in executive management roles in politics, government, or business. However, anyone can be a leader in whatever they are doing both personally and professionally. It's all about how we keep improvising in whatever we have been doing and to find out better and more creative ways to achieve excellence in whatever you are doing.

If we reflect on our life experiences, we notice that leadership opportunities really begin in youth and this is where the most influential leadership life lessons emerge.

We need to be encouraged, supported and nurtured to develop these skills and it should begin in childhood.

As children slowly grow, we all ask them one common question "What would you want to become in life?" In reality, it does not matter what profession they choose in future. What matters is, have they picked up something yet which they are passionate about?

So, through their leadership development we are giving them a chance to identify their true nature, their talents and skills, and enabling them to make their own decisions. All of this is a cumulative effect of qualities which make them bold, confident and above all, a great human being. But yes, we have to keep in mind that they need our support to be able to identify these qualities. Only then, we will have fulfilled our most important duty towards them - helping them discover their purpose of life!

So, looking at the quality of life our children are leading, leadership development is the only way to empower them and teach them how to be responsible and work towards shaping their future.

So, the bottom line is- Are we Leading? Are we leading in our life or being led? Are we leading in our profession? Are we leading as responsible citizen of the country? Are we leading as a Parent or a son or a daughter and so on? This might be a long list but a little awareness and change in your habits and life style can make you lead from the front and you will experience a new life altogether. A life full of possibilities and new opportunities and most important that unbeatable mindset which will keep you going and make your life more meaningful.

2

The Leader in each one of us

Most of us don't see ourselves as leaders whereas the fact is each one of us can develop strong leadership skills through our education, experience and the lessons life teaches us every day.

So, take a trip down the memory lane to remind yourself of all the reasons why you can't be one. Maybe you consider it too late, or you are just too old, too tired or just comfortable in your position right now that you don't want to budge. Stop right there!

The only person stopping you from being one is you. It's never too late for being someone or something. Don't let your mind tell you that you are not capable of anything. Instead, search for that tiny voice that tells you to keep going.

Once you have allowed that voice to direct you, move ahead to plan your goal. No matter how big your goal is, a strategic plan would be needed. And you do not require anyone to do that for you because you know your way around. You know which piece of cake you desire. How you want to use the knife to cut it, is in your hand.

Do not look for advices. Instead, rely on your observation. Others might have achieved success by means that were suitable to them but it might not be the best way for you. We have been oriented differently. Figure that out. You know what works best for you or what you can do about it.

That brings us to another topic called Introspection. Introspection is necessary. Psychologically, introspection is 'the examination or observation of one's own mental and emotional processes'.

Our societies have made us think that financial security is what we need the most. We invalidate other feelings and institutions such as family only to comply to the society's norms. We have set parameters of what should be and what should not be accordingly. We restrain ourselves and others just because it doesn't fit their plan.

Speaking of personal experience, I have come across a lot of clients who had to struggle to get where they are. While there were others who quit their corporate jobs to open a food truck business because they had the passion for cooking and wanted to do something about it. They had to face difficulties and criticism but they were able to cross the bridge.

Most people fail to understand what a leader means. They associate it with competition. A competition is the last thing that is on a leader's mind. They go minding their own business, least bothered about what other people are doing or saying about them. They are the sort of people that genuinely think about other people's wellbeing. They offer help wherever they can and help others progress as well.

To be a leader, you need to develop the mindset that puts you in the shoes of a leader. You have to show commitment to the work you are doing. You have to find your voice. Do not confuse it with being extroverted. Do your job and do it with a lot of energy and passion and improve consistently.

Another tip is to be true to your word. A leader is someone people depend upon. You cannot be the person that does not stand true to their word. Nobody would have remembered Gandhi today if he wouldn't have lived his words. People need someone who genuinely make an effort to keep their words and stick around. Someone who is reliable will always stand out to people.

Never stop working on yourself. There is always room for improvement. The key is to recognize your problem areas. If you have taken the road less travelled, there is a lot of room for exploration and improvement. Do not miss it. We are all creatures looking for our calling. You will find it. Walk down the road with your head held high. Make your own path and others will follow. You are a leader. You will never ask them to follow you. They will do it by themselves.

Build yourself and do not lose touch with the people that matter. Also, always be focused on building contacts. The more people you are open to, the more will revert. It will never hurt to be in contact with someone.

Being a leader does not mean that you throw yourself into work. That is being a workaholic and leaders aren't those.

Leaders are not afraid to change. Neither do they wait for anyone else to come along to make that change. They are the change. You can be too!

3

What Leaders do

What leaders do?

What makes a leader different from a common man is that a leader can raise the ordinary to extra-ordinary. Having said that, quote the pun; ordinary to extra-ordinary which simply indicates that the leaders have all the ordinary qualities that are found in a common man. The only difference is, they magnify and enhance their qualities into virtues. They know how to play on their strengths and practice on their weaknesses. The leader is also a common man bound by human desires and emotions but knows how to rule over and struggle against to get past them. Having said that, almost every person is a leader in his or her own accord, struggling and succeeding his or her way through life taking along with him or her; a team, a family or a squad. It is all but a matter of perspective as to how you want to see something.

- Rational Opinions are something which maximum of the sane fraction of the Homo sapiens seem to have in common. What they lack is the driving force and the correct platform to voice them. In order to change something, initiate or leverage the air of change. Changes will be initiated when you voice your inputs. Such a thing has hugely gained momentum with the advent and widespread use of social media which has immensely helped budding leaders to voice and put forth their opinions and have also made people realize the importance and the perks of voicing their opinions. This will not only benefit them but also benefit the people around them.

- Conversion of sympathy to empathy. When we talk of a common person, we most probably notice that they are sympathetic towards the less fortunate. A common man would donate or help the person who begs for alms or asks for help. A leader is somewhat different. A leader would definitely help the person, no matter, but he understands first that the help is one time the other day would again begin with another dark room shooting struggle. Leaders aim to convert one time helps into life time helps. In such a situation a leader would either try to understand the reason behind the ill fate and try to alleviate the person in need or strive to find a solution. Now this is sympathy with a viable end result; or more so we say, Empathy.
- To move gradually and stealthily from steps to a lunge. No Rome was ever built in a day. Patience is the key. We as a common mass tend to get exhausted or bored pretty easily. No doubt the butter wouldn't start coming up without ample churning. The churning is what makes the task of sticking to it a challenging one. Usually an average person would try a couple of times and then ultimately give up. What makes a leader any different is that, after a couple of tries, he would delve into researching what went wrong each time and find 101 ways in which it won't work but will eventually find that one way which would lead to

success. Baby steps always create a good foundation to build a successful venture.

- The motivation to gain from Individual interests to social interests. As we live in a fairly global community, the issues that almost all of us face, is also global in nature. We won't find sane people littering the streets and the beach. What we do find is that, a majority of people would like to be duty bound and take care of their own wastes. What is a notch higher and rare, is that a person while enjoying the waves of the coast is at the same time, clearing out the clutter someone else has littered? We all would like to scrunch up our noses at the dilapidated condition of our streets and beaches and go as far as complaining and blaming the municipality and at the same time shying away from the taxes and refusing to voice the issues when the polling season begins.

- It all depends on the Perception. Do you see one minute as 60 seconds or one minute as one minute? It all boils down to how you see time. Time is the toughest task master. The one who has mastered the art of managing time is eventually successful. Often, we find people blaming their hectic professional schedules for the lack of exercise and their ill health. Even going to the extents of neglecting their health to such extents that they refuse to have the time to go for a check-up towards an impending health issue. But soon after these specimens of people would swoon over their counterparts commenting how fit and healthy, they are and how well they have maintained themselves. The answer is pretty clear. Diligence and time management is what it takes. Also, priorities dictate a lot of your course of actions. If you are your own priority, leading a pack of wolves is not an issue.

- From shelf control to self-control. A common man tends to regulate matters that are not under his control, but a leader usually aims at controlling himself and knows pretty well that the control anchor on himself will help in maneuvering the control over the situation. We as human beings try to have control over the situation and forget that we are oblivion of what is next to come. What leaders do understand is that if they have control on themselves, the situation partially comes under control through that.
- Time and again we see ourselves making vows and resolutions to ourselves. These vows and resolutions are a good way to keep us grounded, persistent and focused to our goals. But as human nature goes, vows are broken, rules are bent and we get back to our haywire scuttling. It takes a lot of focus and self determination to go through the vows that we make to ourselves. The average population is pretty good at maintaining the vows and resolutions that we have made to others. What makes the leaders different is that, leaders tend to keep their vows to themselves. This should be the level of dedication.
- From reality to clarity. A common man lives and struggles through life. A good leader is one, who has actually felt and experienced life from the scratch. All common men tend to be highly

practical and grounded. Any common man will first accept the reality and then make adjustments and compromises. Leaders tend to bend the axle of fate; they accept the reality, bring clarity to the situation and then work towards achieving their desired results.

- Working for future and living in the present. An average man today has lost the charm of life, working day and night; working for the future. A leader works for the future and toils hard for it, but never forgets to live in the present. The future stocks and resources would be of no use if you do not add emotional value to it in the present. A major chunk of adult life is spent on education or professional life, where the major compromises are faced by personal life. What we fail to realize is that, we earn to have a good and comfortable personal life, but of late that life doesn't even seem to exist.
- From thinking out of the box, to thinking of what to do with the box. As the age-old adage goes, think out of the box. Usually no one does think of what to do with the box. A common man does try his best to make all out of his scarce resources, but usually fails to realize or acknowledge his potential resources or turns a blind eye towards them. Leaders on the other hand while making the best out of their resources, also try to pin point their potential resources. In short, they can see potential without credentials.
- From making ends meet to stretching limits. We as commoners are great in adjusting and stretching

resources to make both ends meets. We are the best practitioners of making the most even from the lost. Leaders are no less; they use this similar virtue to stretch themselves beyond their comfort level. This is why we see that many impossible tasks have turned into "They are Possible!"

We are all the same, it only depends on what we want to intensify, what we want to work for and how we want to lead ourselves. Remember, Leadership isn't about telling people what to do, it's first living it yourself, and others following by example.

4

What's your Big why

What's your big why?

It was the evening before Christmas and Jackie was still confused as to what he should ask Santa for? He was almost 12 years old and yet somehow believed in the age-old tales and folklores. Much to amazement, the tales and folklores seemed to respond him back in ways unfathomable to common perception. After much contemplation and several crumpled sheets later, he wrote a letter to him.

Dear Santa,

I had been a good boy all the year round. I also bagged the first prize in the running race and scored good marks in my tests as well. I have obeyed my parents every day and fed the street dogs everyday back from school. I am so sorry for I lied once to mom, that the wind broke the vase, otherwise Snowy would have been punished for that accidental crash. She did nothing intentionally.

I don't want any Christmas present this year, just wanted to know, what makes you so special? Am I special too? Why am I doing all good things? Hope you write me back.

Love,

Jackie

And with this he closed the letter, put it near the chimney and went to bed.

At midnight, his father tiptoed his way to the chimney bottoms to retrieve Jackie's and Snowy's letters. Snowy had asked for a pet dog and dog food for it.

"Guess this wish needs to be postponed." He hummed under his breath.

Opening Jackie's Letter, he began reading it. He was amazed by the child's sensitivity and curiosity. He decided it was time to quench his curiosity and give him some insight into the depths and roots of life. Next morning, Jackie woke up and ran straight to the socks, hung above the chimneys if Santa had come to take his letters. To his surprise, the letter was gone and there was a huge tumble-roll wooden Santa doll, with a spherical base, resting inside the socks with a letter. He quickly opened the letter and was about to read it, when his father came down.

"Good morning son, anything special this year? What did Santa leave for you?"

"Oh Dad! Look here! I got this really Cute Santa Doll that rolls around. Isn't it huge? You see the furrowed eyebrows and the frown resting on him? I wonder how big real Santa might be? And yeah, I got this letter as well, its long though."

> "Want me to read it out for you?"
> "Sure, Dad that would be awesome." And his father started reading.

Dear Jackie,

I am so glad; you did so well the entire year. You have been such a good boy and to reward you, I shall answer your questions, and as we are in this together, we need to be good friends. But before that you have to tell what do you see in that doll that I have left for you? Isn't it just huge and intimidating? Just the way I look and the way you picturize me. Isn't it?

Well, go ahead, open the doll. Did you open it? I shall know, if you won't so go and open it.

"Let's open the doll son."

Jackie twists the doll in its middle and it splits into two parts, removing the head and torso from the wobbly rounded base. The doll reveals another doll of Santa inside, sporting a jolly smile and happy eyes smirking and smiling with an ear-splitting curve on his lips.

His father reads again.

Well if you opened it, you shall see that I am downright jolly. I make merry and have fun and oblige myself to the almighty for all the precious moments, opportunities to serve children and happiness I receive in life. But that's not it, there's more. Now open again.

This time, Jackie was excited to see what was inside. The twisted open the jolly doll, to find a Mysterious expression on the face of the third doll. The eyes were scrutinizing and an eyebrow was perked upwards and he seemed right unfathomable.

The letter further read.

The mystery is what makes me so invincible. No one knows my next move. This makes me more interesting, more longed for. Mysterious is what makes you difficult to read and shields you from vulnerability. You know what you are supposed to do next, now go ahead, twist.

Opening the third doll, a bit smaller, medium sized doll was revealed. The expression was aggressive, lethal and sported a courageous outlook. The eyes were focusing with rage and valor.

God will never let you face anything that you can't handle of your own. Assistance is always provided to people who deserve it. Just always remember to be fearless. Face your problems, but first of all acknowledge your fears and face them, to conquer them.

Time for the twist.

Twisting open the fourth doll, a little doll was revealed, from the inside. The expression was soft, the eyes were baby like and the heart was seen through the red Santa coat. It looked like a real softy; a baby Santa but with all white beards and a chubby expression.

When you get to know me deeper, I care. I am caring and I listen to anyone who needs me in their hour of distress. Caring and love is the key to a fruitful life. When you spread love and show it through your care, that makes you a person worth the creation of God. I know you are excited, grab the last click.

Jackie was brimming with curiosity now. He hastily opened the little doll, but couldn't exactly see anything inside. He poured down the contents onto his palms when a miniature infant Santa, with no beard and absolutely baby blue big eyes was revealed. The miniature doll was clad in red drapes and looked up at the onlooker with curiosity and amazement.

And now my child, this is my center. I have big eyes. Eyes that see the wonder in everything. Eyes that are full of wonder and amazement. This is what I was born with, eyes that have seen only wonder in everything, everybody and every moment. Eyes that see light in the trees and magic in the air. Wonder is what I put into the world and what I protect in children and human beings. This is what makes me special, makes me the guardian of the world. It is my big why, the why with which I was born, and the why for which I have served centuries.

I told you mine, now what's yours?

You are a bright young child, my love. You will grow up to be an amazing person one day. Let your layers reveal and find your center. I'll be back next year, till then, start counting and revealing your layers. The core isn't much deep.

Love,

Santa.

So, the moral of the story is:

- The real us is buried very deep inside us.
- The years of social and mental conditioning, the rules of the society and the demand of the situation creates several layers of attributes around us, to sheath us from vulnerability.
- A person in order to reach their core, and determine their purpose, have to first, cut through the layers that we have built through the years, subconsciously.
- It is always not necessary that you put into the world what you are asked to contribute. You subconsciously contribute what you are best at. It is the love and passion towards an activity that connects you to it. Go for it. That's your core.

- It doesn't matter what profession you follow. If you know what you ache for and work towards meeting your heart's longing, you are on the right path.
- The meaning of life is to find your gift. To find that purpose, so big, that it practically challenges every fiber of your being to deliver the best of you.
- Do not be distracted by comparison when you are captured with a purpose that works as your driving force. If you can't stop thinking about it, then don't stop working towards it either.
- Things that excite your soul and your subconscious are not random things. They are connected to your purpose. Follow them.

The two most important days of a person's life, are the day when he was born and the day, they find out why. Find a purpose to serve, not a lifestyle to live. Your life is your message to the world.

5

Leadership Begins at home

Leadership indeed begins at home. You would not even realize that your children, your spouse, your parents and your relatives are watching every move of yours. They are constantly learning or want to learn from you. especially your children. If you are his/her elder brother or sister, your siblings are also constantly watching you and they look up to you as you are an integral part of their world.

So, what matters the most is, how we act at home and how we deal with things at home. There are people who are super-duper at work or in the outside world however when it comes to home, they take it very easy.

We as parents want the best for our children; right from balanced diet to a healthy environment; from quality education to best mentors, from a good society to a good leader, we keep ticking off the points in our checklist. Our initiation and investment in our children are of utmost importance when it comes to raising them as socially responsible individuals. Being a parent in the 21st century; comes with great leadership responsibilities. We get to vote and chose our leaders but our children have no such option. They look up to us as their leader and their role models in the early days of their life and we as parents have to make sure we stand up to their future developmental requirements. Clearly, leadership begins at home and there are a few facets that every parent should go through in the journey of leading their child towards a brighter realm in life.

Leading children is like potter's clay, you mould them, shape them and also fill them. It's three times more the responsibility than that of leading a team of adults and professionals.

Clear, effective and non-judgmental communication among the members of the family paves the way towards the growth of a rational, logical and open -minded individual. The more you communicate with your children, the more you encourage the flow of ideas and information. This not only piques their interest and curiosity but also helps them imbibe different facets to a subject. It somehow helps you to get a sneak- peek into the mental pastures of the child and gives you a better opportunity to prune the tree before it's too late. Welcome the opinions what your children provide, accept and appreciate if they seem to be good enough. If you reject the opinions, give them reasons for it along with tips to be better at them. This will help the child be an effective and a rational communicator which is a skill inherent to leaders. Shuffle roles when it is needed, be a parent and a friend both; because good leaders are good guides but great friends for people who follow them.

It's strange how love and empathy can replace bossing and ordering around which makes leadership a much easier task at hand back at home. Not only does it inspire to be gentler and more understanding but also leads to a more level headed individual. A good leader always puts himself in the shoes of whom he leads and takes decision that would provide an enriched experience to his followers. Only with love and empathy can a person test, stretch and reach limits, at the same time learning how to set and achieve desirable goals.

It takes confidence and courage in an individual to take responsibility and accountability for the tasks they are entitled to. "Any challenge can be undertaken and won, with a positive attitude." This should be the mantra. Neither encourage, nor practice playing the blame game with your child or with other family members. Take accountability for your actions and decisions and notice the child follow suit. Instead of playing a blame game, make sure the child has his roles and rules chart prepared. When achievable targets are not being met, look for loopholes, encourage or penalize as the situation and attitude demands. Small household chores are a good way to inculcate such attitudes in children. Sibling relationships play a great role in the responsibility sector as well.

The apple doesn't fall far from the tree. It's amazing how our children turn out to be so much like us, both consciously and subconsciously. This also brings to light as to how careful we should be regarding ourselves as leaders. Parents have an immense influence over their children and leadership works on the lifeline of influence. Honesty, integrity, focus and humility make for good influencers in your child. In the future, the influence of your child would affect his friend circle and being a socially responsible parent, we owe this to our society. There would be no greater responsibility as leaders than to paint the picture of the future generation and shape them to be the next leaders in making. Be a leader with a vision, and make sure your child accepts that vision, only then will you be able to achieve your goals as a family. These things need to be started early, if not it is easy to expect clashes in mentality and ideologies.

A leader is known for his focus, consistency and continuous hard work for a common cause. Being fickle minded and indecisive with regular change of plans along with lack of planning makes for an uncoordinated and messed up mentality. These are undesirable traits for any human being let alone a leader. Farsightedness and proper planning, with provisions for emergencies, are some of the qualities that your child should notice in you as a parent and learn from it. Traits like this increase the reliability quotient of the followers on their leaders and it also sets a good example to your child. The more resourceful a planner you are, the more reliability you acquire. You as a parent, while portraying such traits would encourage your children to acquire the same. The way a smile is infectious, so are virtues. Once your child picks up these traits and actually starts to implement them in his day to day life, in his school, in his playground, with his siblings, on his study table and practically in every sector and phase of his life; you have succeeded yourself as a leader.

Leadership is not something that is taught or injected. It is developed, it is inculcated and a real leader lives this life through and through every day. A leader is not only the one who leads the nation or the one with a million followers, it starts with the base of the society, and that is your family, my family, everybody's family. Our homes are the nurturers to all the potential leaders of tomorrow, let's equip them for a better tomorrow.

6
Leadership at work

The only place where success comes before work is in the dictionary. Ruling with an iron fist is only going to crash you down like a lead balloon. Your workplace is the second most prominent place of your life, where you spend most of your time. Leading your way through your professional life either you are in a job or in business is one the most important skills that have to be inculcated by a person. Your work place could be a battlefield, a roadside kitchen, a corporate enclosure or a recycle shack; it hardly matters, as long as the workplace keeps operating as your source of bread you need to win over the place. Being a boss and being a leader are two very different things. You might not be the boss but you sure can be a leader. It is not necessary that whoever the boss is; is the leader. Leader is about action, not position. Its about what you do and not about what you have. In order to be a leader in your workplace, you have to start leading yourself first, the way you carry yourself, the surety of your actions and decisions will create an aura of confidence around you.

During my first job in the corporate sector, I had this really prominent co-worker who was also my supervisor and had her way of getting things done. She wanted her notes a particular way, cell phones on silent and it was as if she was the living embodiment of discipline and particularity. I really didn't like the way she needed everything prim and proper. She did try to delegate me in different phases but I was too unwilling to budge.

On one fine morning, we were having our espressos and I could see that one of my co-workers came and asked her to help him out on a Task. Though she was busy with her own work, she gave her the outlines along with Documentation to perform the task. He was back again the next day, with another topic which my supervisor gladly assisted with. This went on for a couple of more days; every morning, my supervisor would reserve a good ten minutes for the new joinee. Though he apologized every morning for taking her time, yet my supervisor held no grudge towards him. One morning, he didn't come to our booth and my supervisor voluntarily sent me in search for him as to what the matter might be. I made a trip round the office but found no traces of him. I could hear faint conversations from the Director's Cabin who was our Super boss.

"Your business is not going the right way as it should go and the turnover is very low. I need more funds and if you cannot do that for me, I have others that would do that for me. Either you achieve your targets this very month or you will be fired." I knew it was him inside the cabin, and went to inform my supervisor. I told her whatever I made out of the faint conversation I heard and she asked me to take a seat. The afternoon passed in a blurry with no other event when our Super boss called her along with me to take notes. He indeed was firing him due to his low business turnover and asked my supervisor to start searching for a replacement within one month's notice.

She agreed readily to his commands before speaking again;

"Sir, I do agree that he had not been doing very well but I can assure you that currently finding a replacement and training him would be a lot costlier as it is almost midyear. I have gone through his profile and background and have also interacted with him. And I know exactly where the problem lies."

I could see that our Super boss was annoyed at her for taking his side, but at the same time it piqued his interest as to what was the problem that she could detect. Out of curiosity he asked, "And what would that be, if I may ask?"

"You see, he was a late entrant and had got no high-level corporate training before he joined our office, he has a really good basic and foundation but doesn't know how to operate our software, due to which his business is getting a hit and his efficiency is reduced. If you allow me, I would like to see where he goes in a month, operating under me. I will keep searching for candidates in the meanwhile and at the end of the month, you can decide for yourself. I guess he will catch up in a month and adding another joinee will only add one month to the launch pad."

After a moment of thoughtful contemplation, the creases and furrows on his forehead relaxed and out he spoke, "Take a month, either ready him to perfection or find me another."

"I won't disappoint you sir."

And for the next one month I was left on my own, to sit by the couch or work under other people and their projects while that guy took my seat next to my supervisor.

I was asked to take regular progress tabs and make graphs of his progress. And soon it was a matter of a bit less than a month that he over achieved his target. And for me, I had a head start on three different topics all of which intrigued me and working with different topics and people reduced the monotonicity of the work.

It was almost the end of the month and I could see the employee of the month going to the new joinee who was once about to be fired by the Super boss. I completed my internship successfully under my supervisor and also got an offer to join under her and I was more than glad to accept.

Being in her vicinity taught me a few things that a true leader should inculcate in their day to day work place practices.

So, what can we learn from this story which will help us to lead @ Work:

- Be an avid listener. In today's world everyone just loves to talk. However, Listening is the key to information. She used to listen to whoever came to ask for help and that's what made her so approachable. She was open to a healthy discussion and was always open to learning and sharing. Remember, **when you talk you are only repeating what you already know, but when you listen, you may learn something new.**
- An eye for detail was what made her unique in the crowd. She did not ever help for the sake of helping or charity. She made sure that the person was worth helping and what was the reason behind the need to be helped.
- She was a very tactful communicator and knew which buttons to push in order to get a desired answer. Clear, efficient and effective

communication is the key to good leadership practice.
- Be courageous to speak up for the right, but always wait for your turn to speak. Speaking out of turn may ruin your chances of success. But speak out when it is necessary to speak. Do not speak if you cannot add value to silence.
- Far sightedness is ability with leaders. They can smell talent from a distance and gauge its intensity and make sure which resources would they fulfil. Interact freely with people in order to enhance such skills.
- Try to make decisions that would benefit the team/community as a whole rather than just thinking of the gains. After all, you are what your decisions portray about you.
- Never hesitate to share or gain knowledge. Always opt for a healthy and hearty competition. You might not win but you will certainly learn.
- Never play the game of favoritism; it will eventually lead to biasness which is a complete disaster for a leader.
- Take responsibility for your actions and only take them if you are sure that you are capable enough to carry them out.
- Don't micromanage all the time.

Leading Vs Micromanaging

Good human relation skills have the ability to change people from managing others to leading others. If polls are to be believed, no employee has ever asked to be micromanaged. Micromanagement is a style of management which is completely different from any sort of healthy leadership practices. Leadership is more about relying on your followers, creating more leaders rather than humanoid robots, programmed to follow instructions and complete tasks. Whilst both the approaches have their own pros and cons, micromanaging certainly has a darker taint to it when it comes to acceptance by common employees and practitioners.

- Micromanaging works wonders for small scale companies which need constant supervision as their initial steps are essential to build the future foundation in the long run of success. No doubt. Fall, get up and start sounds all so motivational; but new start-ups and small-scale companies do not have sufficient funds to absorb the shocks of crashing. In such cases, micromanaging is very helpful and also helps in proof reading and cross checking of day to day operations and targets.
- Where as in leadership, the same situation is more into efficient delegation and supervision. No doubt a leader will also go through the day's progress in terms of results accomplished but will also rely on the operation and supervision of his employees and followers without personally going through them all over.
- Micromanaging is at times a very tedious process, which consumes time, energy, manpower and money. While leadership is passion, micromanaging is often an obsession. As it is said, too much of anything is bad, likewise; too much of managing will lead to obsession to protocols, there by leading

to unnecessary exploitation of resources that could have been channelized to some better avenues.
- Leadership as such lets followers to explore and outsource and make optimum use of time and resources.
- Micromanaging assures the uniformity and quality that is needed for branding in the initial days of a product or service launch. It also ensures accuracy and result orienteers of a given action and event.
- Leadership allows creativity to flow and create a path, whilst micromanaging aims at following a well pre-defined path and deviations are usually frowned at. Hence, leadership can be more beneficial for avenues looking for change, development, creativity and innovation, whereas micromanaging is more useful in quality assurance, branding and feature oriented products, that demand uniformity in services.
- Micromanaging gives a sense of control to the manager in charge. It somehow takes the accountability and responsibility, off the shoulders of the employees, making it a liability on the part of the manager.
- Leadership is always preferred in the long run when the actions can no longer be closely monitored and delegation becomes an important part of managing day to day operations. It gives a power of responsibility and accountability to followers or employees who in turn learn to be accountable for their own actions. On the other hand, if we talk of micromanaging, the dynamics somewhat change.

- While leadership is more of action and passion oriented, micromanaging is more result and feedback oriented. With micromanaging, constant feedbacks can be given to the employees at work. A stitch in time saves nine. Problems from the very beginning can be detected, before they turn out to be huge problems in future. Micromanagement divides the final result into various instalments that are to be delivered in specific time periods. This determines a constant work flow and also gives an indication towards the progress of the project or employee.
- This doesn't mean leadership is not result oriented. The difference is, leadership is more of long-term result oriented, while micromanagement is short term or periodic result oriented. Leadership is like carving the path and letting your followers decide the pace and the camps.

Advantages of Micromanaging

- We often hire smart people so that they can give us solutions when the company needs them. This theory proves somewhat dysfunctional when it comes to micromanaging. Howsoever smart the employee may be, smartness will never undermine the procedural protocols. Micromanaging works best for employees who are low on confidence or are new to field who need constant guidance, advices and supervision to make it through the end. It is not an easy job to keep an eye on anything and everything now a days and when your boss or manager actually keeps an eye on your progress, then it is a good deal to take in. Micromanaging might sound harsh to the employee but it is equally harsh on the manager as well.

- An eye to detail is what makes a micromanager a successful manager. Many start-ups prefer micromanagers due to this very characteristic feature of this management style. Whatever the venture may be, long term or short term, all leaders, managers, projects, missions and even teams, face one thing in common; competition. It is not always necessary that competition turns out to be healthy. When competition turns messy, instances of spying, cheating, information exporting and other such cases are very common. A micromanaging firm or team can easily detect such cases in no time. This makes the firm doubly protected from intruders. In leadership, however the only things that can prevent such occurring are the presence of mind of the leader and the network of faithful employees and followers who work for him. Usually such cases are noticed quicker in case of micromanagement.
- Constant know how of performance consistency and knowledge of business risks are some of the added benefits of micromanagement.

In today's date, if a healthy discussion is to be made, the highest polls would go to leadership than to micromanagement. The reason being, despite all benefits, micromanagement still weighs down, in terms of space, freedom, creativity and employee retention. Micromanaging can be done in a short-term basis in combination to certain leadership practices, but it must be avoided as soon as chances of expansion and long-term benefits begin to light the horizon. It is good to have passion for perfection but it must be checked for obsession to stagnation.

7

Are you leading by example?

Great leaders don't tell you what to do; they show you how it's done. A boss drives, but a leader coaches. By walking your talk, you make people trust and believe in your words. It leads to a motivation that etches into the mind of your followers and your co-workers. Always remember a leader works and strives towards a goal carved out of a vision; but a boss targets a number. Anything is possible with the right amount of diligence, talent and perseverance. There is a fine line of distinction between reasonable goals and unrealistic targets. And more importantly it is really essential to have a solid path and planned structure carved out in order to achieve those reasonable goals which might have once seemed to be impossible.

Little acts of virtue and excellence can set an example before the people in general or children to follow a path less travelled these days. I still remember during my school days, when we were given points for our social work activities wherein, we contributed an hour every Saturday morning, planting and watering plants. It usually happened that none of our plants would survive for more than three weeks. After a couple of months of our failed attempts, our class teacher who was a real strict lady with round spectacles advised us to water them every morning. Owing to her pointed glare we did that for a week and gradually fell out of habit again and this time the plants survived a little more than the third week before withering away.

Saturday came rolling again and new saplings were planted and watered. Next Monday, as we entered the school compound, we could see Mrs Patro, with her round glasses down, watering our saplings. We could see droplets of water splattered across the hems of her attire which meant she had been doing this since a good while. It wasn't polite to watch your teacher work when you are around, so we offered her our help and all the saplings were watered before the assembly started. The next day, the school compound greeted us with the same view again and once more, manners took over. This time we were joined by some more of our classmates. Every morning we looked forward to watering plants with Mrs Patro, and in a few weeks' time, the entire class was doing it with her. By the end of the session, all the plants had survived with absolutely no casualties.

In due course of time, students from other classes and corridors had started mimicking us, along with the respective class teachers. Not only did it save the saplings, but also taught us that consistency can lead to successful results. And a long line of tradition followed even after we passed out from our schools, the successors have followed suit. I went to my school last year for an alumni meet, and I could still see Mrs Patro's saree hem, wet with droplets of water.

This might have been a significantly moderate step on behalf of Mrs Patro to initiate and enforce responsibility and consistency in efforts for what we do as developing children. But what I realized was that, in her actions she taught us, nothing that she wouldn't do herself, which was in a way leadership by example. And not only that, after we had developed a habit, she still continued it with us and for years later, even after us. This shows the inherent quality of leadership in her to carry on the work that she has started and not just give up.

Leading by example is not a tough task at hand.

Be one amongst the crowd. Do not hesitate to do something that would demonstrate or set a good example among your followers and people. When you consider yourself, one among the many, you are able to empathize and be more compassionate towards your followers and also it helps you to keep a check on your progress and the pace of the project at hand. Being one of them will fraternize you to them. When they see you performing, they will be motivated to follow suit. Be a role model by actually modelling for a task.

Deliver results with excellence. Be consistent in your approach, one-time demonstration will always wither away the effect. Go over, under and around the hurdles to make sure nothing can stop you and your endeavors towards your goal. Walk through the fire yourself first to make sure you are not sabotaging your followers and team in the process of striving towards your purpose. This will instill trust in their minds for you.

Be truthful and responsible for your own actions, accept failures if it is needed. Blame game will only cost you your credibility and your trustworthiness, killing the real progress graph in the long run. Inaccurate representations will lead to confusion, conflict, losses, weak team dynamics and a weak morale. Follow, practice and prove that honesty is ultimately the best policy at hand.

Respect the chain of command, at every level. A leader at any level is still a leader. Do not mess around with direct reporting. Respect boundaries at every level. This will let the departments have independent space to work and also will foster good and viable leadership practices among the various budding leaders. Respect head of all departments, both with and without the team's presence.

Choose your battles wisely. It is a remarkable quality in an individual to know what to fight for, when to fight for, how much to fight for and most importantly knowing when to stop fighting for. Channelizing you and your team's energy, into something productive can greatly boost their morale after being successful as the ultimate goal is the reward. Do not fight a raging battle if you don't gain anything by winning. It is ok if you do not land a treasure while digging the mountain; you at least made a way to the other side to explore opportunities.

Effective leaders lead by example, with honesty, confidence and compassion employing intelligence and humor. SAY IT, DO IT AND LIVE IT!

8

Are you struggling right now?

The challenge and struggle you are in today is developing the strength you need for tomorrow. I had once been to this fancy-dress competition of my son, when he was still wearing size 1 shoes. The opening ceremony had a dance program by the toddler section. There were a group of children on the lit stage and the occasional shuffling of the positions could be clearly heard from behind the curtains. The curtains began to pull apart, when suddenly the lights went off. Being toddlers, this led to a cacophony of tears and wails before the backup power supply was put on. The lights were back, and the toddlers somewhat calmed down, but no amount of coaxing or mimicking could make them dance anymore. They tried to play the music many a time, but the dance really didn't seem to start or coordinate anymore. A little girl was still afraid and frowning at the back. Her tears were relentlessly falling though her wailing and sobs were gone.

Just then, one of the spectators went up to the stage from the crowd, and spoke something to the music operator. He went to the back of the stage to stand with the little frightened girl and as soon as the music started, the man started dancing alongside the little girl. I guess he was probably her father. Soon after the man started dancing, after a good 20 seconds the girl stopped shedding her tears and started dancing along with him. The dance had probably begun, the crowd was astonished now. Seeing the girl dance, some of the other toddlers started moving as well. But the man did not stop he kept dancing with the little girl. Soon after he was joined by another parent who accompanied and urged his son to dance who was standing perplexed on the stage. After a good one minute of this, the crowd of parents gradually started mimicking the steps to encourage the children to move and dance.

The round of dance ended and the song was played again where all the children and the parents danced together and enjoyed themselves. What could once have been a cancelled show, had now become a full-fledged mass drill of laughter, enjoyment and success. When asked to the little girl's father, he said

"This was my daughter's first dance! When she grows up, I couldn't show a video of her, wailing and spoiling her make up on stage. She will grow up to be a princess, a successful one, and that starts from now. If it demands me to be with her on stage then I will be with her in every path to lead and edge her on!"

One of the other parents who followed suite next to him, commented, "What example would I set to my child, if instead of encouraging and being a parent, I chose to be a spectator who just gave sympathy. Being spectacular would always count more than being a spectator."

"It felt good to support my child! I never knew doing such a small thing would encourage him! I would definitely do this from now on. After all he has got just one set of parents to look up to. I want to be there for him always." commented another.

It is very much evident that not all the people can be leaders. If all of them are leaders, there won't be any followers and that would lead to a conflict of positions and ideas as well. We can also see this from another perspective; that different people are leaders in different genres of life. Some are spiritual and emotional leaders, some are leaders in their household and personal space, and some are leaders in their friends and acquaintance circle, where as some as leaders in the professional and political forefront, and some lead in the social forefront. From the scenario above, we can contemplate that there were three major parts to how the event turned upside down.

- The power cut led to an unseen hindrance to the event and no amount of shock absorbers from the sponsors could do any damage control. The parent with an idea/solution came forward which worked; making him a kind of a leader of the mass event.
- The second and the most important person was the second person that joined him. He was the actual crowd puller, counting as the first follower. He was an encouragement and enthusiasm to the crowd that would soon follow.
- With the people following suit, the rest had to come up, as they are used to being a part of the crowd and would not like to be left alone.

Most of the people are usually in a dilemma whether they should lead or should they follow. And that gradually turns into an internal struggle.

- In order to clear out this dilemma, one has to make sure what he or she actually wants, to create a change or to help create a change. One has to find their genre. One can lead in a particular field, only when he or she actually feels passionate towards

the cause. It is a process of self-awareness where only you can determine whether you can create the blue prints or can you reinforce the walls and lay the bricks, the decision is completely up to you.
- If you want to lead, recognize your vision and your driving force. It is not easy to find the cause that would drive you as well as others enough so to make them follow you.
- Treat your first followers as your equal, they have a great deal of contribution in your crowd pulling in your initial times.

When we talk about following, we usually get a picture of the rat race, but that is not the case. If you are sure enough that you have the persistence and resources but not the direction to work towards something, you should really try following but chose well.

- A follower is what makes the visionary a leader. Without a good follower, or a crowd puller a leader does not really exist.
- Followers form the base of the team and they help the leader achieve the goals and work towards the vision. Shah Jahan initiated the construction of Taj Mahal, but it was actually built by the 20,000 workers who had lost their fingers in that process. The success of a leader depends on his followers as much as it depends on him.
- As the saying goes, be a good follower if you want to become a good leader; being a follower will help you walk in their shoes which are really important to fathom once you become a leader.

Real leaders do not create followers; they create more leaders at heart and soul.

9

Leading in tough times

Hard times do not create heroes. It is during the hard times that the hero within us is revealed. Being a leader is all about taking responsibility, of yourself as well as your followers.

There is this story which I personally had a fondness to, during the early days of my childhood. But I would narrate it in my own version. I never actually liked its ending, so I would usually cook up various endings before drifting off to sleep.

A mischief of mice resided in the dark alleys and corners of the kitchen in a large palace. One day, the little three-year-old princess of the castle was strolling through the royal garden, when suddenly her tummy rumbled.

"Grrrr"

"I am so hungry." Complaining, she darted straight towards the royal kitchen. It was deserted and no chef or cook were visible in plain sight.

"How am I going to get muffins?" she grumbled to herself.

A smell of freshly baked cake, wafted to her nostrils.

"Wow, that's a pineapple pie." And her little feet made their way to the direction of the delicious aroma. She opened the cupboard when a shrill cry left her throat.

"Aaaaaaaaaah"

Out there in front of her, were three mice, all fat and plump feasting on a small piece of the pineapple pie. The mice, equally frightened, witnessing a giant human in front of them, screaming in all her might, scuttled in all directions.

Clang!

It so happened that the princess in her frenzied state of fright, tripped over a mouse and fell headlong into the drum of raspberry sorbet, bruising an arm and her chin, with a rat-trap clinging to her beautiful golden hair. The chefs and the maids ran into the kitchen gasping in awe; the bedlam unfolding before them.

"Your Highness, let me help you." Said the maid; as she helped the princess to her feet. By that time rivulets of tears were streaming down the cheeks of the princess and the royal stewards carried her to her bedroom, where the King and the Queen were furious with anger. The rat trap was carefully removed from her hair, taking away with it, a tuft full of golden locks. The Royal Healer was called for and after the princess was treated, fed and taken care of; the King and the Queen called for a meeting.

"Our palace has been infested with these filthy rodents. The matter has gotten out of our hands. I will take absolutely no chances with the health and safety of my angel. All rat-traps are to be removed from this very instant. It's my order that all rodents in the Royal Kitchen are to be caught and killed within a week. All servants are to be deployed to this task" The King announced.

"But your majesty, Servants wouldn't be able to squeeze themselves into rat holes and sacks. I would rather suggest you to adopt a cat, which would be more suitable. It would be a good pet to our princess and also the pet will enjoy a good hunt. No mice would dare venture near the princess. The cat can hunt mice when the princess is unavailable." The Queen suggested, as all the maids and servants let out a sigh of relief.

Next day, the princess could be seen strutting along with a big, fat, whiskered, fluffy white kitten; the events of the previous day, all forgotten. With the princess happy with the kitten, the weather of the palace turned to spring again. But the dark alleyways of the palace had some other story to narrate.

All the mice of the palace held a meeting. Their numbers were dwindling. Every day they were losing a friend.

"She moves so stealthily," said one mouse

"Her footsteps can't even be heard," said another. "She catches us by surprise," added another; and on

they went describing her cunning moves.

The old mouse was listening to all this. They mice community always looked up to him for any advice and suggestions. With expectant eyes they looked up to him, even the chief himself sought his advice.

"We should tie a bell to her neck," said the old mouse, "when she moves, the ringing bell would warn us of her arrival."

The mice whooped at the idea cheering and applauding, except the chief. After the whoops died, he finally raised his question, "Your age has started to take over your mind, old mouse! Your suggestion is valid but it's impossible and useless. Who will bell the cat? And that too without being killed! We can't afford to lose more numbers. And we are not even sure if that will be a successful attempt. This isn't a good idea; we have to think of something different. Maybe, leave the palace and search for a new abode. Some of us can migrate to our relatives in the town."

The silence was deafening, as if, it was a graveyard, and even the spirits were asleep. Even the breaths could not be heard.

"I'll do it," squeaked the smallest of them. He was gaunt and scrawny, often bullied by his mates for being a fancy inventor and plotter. He was one of the many few mice who had joined them after the town was devastated in the famine.

"You?"

"Leave it to me. Just get me a few bells and a ribbon," squeaked the little one. "We came here in expectation of a better life, we can't leave this place, and it's our home. Life outside is even shittier. Either ways we are going to die. If the cat doesn't kill us, then hunger will. Why not try my best? I'll fight for our existence. In the afternoon, when the brute is fed and satisfied, I'll tie the bell around her neck."

In the afternoon, after lunch, the cat lazily moved into the bedroom near the kitchen and hopped onto the stool, admiring herself in the dressing mirror.

"How so beautiful you are. There is no other cat as beautiful as you that I have ever seen." She heard a voice. She turned around to see a little grey mouse bowing down at her.

Are We Leading?

She was flattered with his words and blushed at his compliment. Also, her stomach was full.

"You seem to be a wise mouse," she complimented.

"Wise, yes, but not beautiful, like you, your Majesty," he complimented some more to make it real.

The cat looked at herself in the mirror again, admiring her white fur; when he spoke again.

"How much prettier would you look if your pretty neck were had a necklace."

"But where would I get a necklace from? The princess doesn't let me wear none," The cat complained.

"Do you mean something like this?" the little mouse held the bell necklace and smiled slyly at her.

"Oh, my goodness, it is so pretty." The cat jumped, to snatch it from him. For a split second he was taken off guard thinking she might pounce on him but quickly regained his composure.

"Your Majesty, I am your admirer from the day you arrived, would you mind, if I tie this around your neck?"

As the cat's stomach was full, she had a surge of love for the little mouse who has presented her with the most beautiful necklace she could ever wear. The little mouse tied it around her neck making sure the knots were abundant and the necklace had no chance to be loose to come off her neck. With a last bow, he retreated to his gathering, where he was welcomed as a hero with whoops and claps of appreciation.

The cat admired herself the entire afternoon in front of the mirror. Her tummy rumbled in the evening and she went in search of mice in the kitchen, but to her awe, she could find none, all the mice scuttled away to their rat holes, even before she could set foot towards them.

Leadership is not just about position. It is about leading when your people need you the most.

- There will be problems everywhere. Remember your vision, why you started the thing that you started. It is easy to start something and leave something midway. But always finish what you started. Switching to something better doesn't guarantee that there would be no challenges. If you want to achieve something, you have to be capable and prove yourself that you are worthy of it. Only challenges that come along the way, equip you as a leader who can handle the success that comes at the end of the tunnel. Face off the problem.
- Do not lose hope. If there is a will, there is a way. Always look at every facet of the problem. Do not just fret as you look at the problem and run head long to the exit door. Instead plot ways so that the problem runs through the exit doors.
- Know your vision, and know the problems that come with it. Every coin has two sides. When you start working on something, weigh the pros and cons. Plan and carve the path for the pros, but make back up and emergency plans for the cons. You can only lead in tough times, when you are well equipped with all your resources. Keep your friends close, but your enemies, even closer. Plan according to the demand of the situation.
- Being a leader, it is your responsibility to contain the fear in yourself and not to let the fear seep into

the minds of the followers. The battle is lost if fear creeps into your minds, leading to hopelessness and defeat. Always find ways to keep the spirits high and keep up the positivity among the people around you.

- Do not lose your stance and wits. Your composure will be your greatest asset as a leader. Keep your senses open and keep an eye for details. A calm and composed mind is a reservoir of productive ideas and split-second decisions.
- It is always easy to reject suggestions, but there are times when suggestions might not give you all the answers. There are many ways to approach a problem. Evaluate the best possible alternative with bare minimum casualties and losses. As a leader it is your responsibility to convert the impossible into possible; and that's what makes you the leader.
- Accept what the followers have to suggest. If it is possible, act on them. A good leader always understands and accepts his followers when times are adverse. If they trust you in their times of distress, you should also trust them with your confidence.
- Confidence and creativity are the key to thrive a taxing situation. Your confidence reflects in your speech and radiates from your personality. Confidence gives you courage. Nothing can be more welcome than courage in dire situations of treat and distress.

Brick walls aren't there to keep us out, they are there to give us a chance to show how badly we want something and who cares for it enough to tear it down.

10

Leading by your values

When your values are clear to you, making decisions becomes easier. The decisions we make are a reflection of our core values and ethics and they are directed towards a specific goal. That specific goal may refer to satisfaction of either personal or collective needs of people involved. When our values govern our decisions, we make a subconscious choice; as to what is important to us. When the tunnel of life goes dark, your values will be the torch to lighten it up and lead the way. The light at the end of the tunnel is real; the tunnel is your illusion.

- One of the core leadership values that must be earned and given is respect. Every human being regardless of his position and status must be treated with the respect that he or she deserves. A good leader always respects the people who are working for him. With love and respect even the toughest of nuts flip open like sea shells. Respect is not asked for, it has to be earned, and mere acquisition of position does not guarantee the level of respect. Respect is something which is a mutual process if studied in a true sense.
- In order to prove oneself, one has to work towards making a difference in the society. Making a difference largely depends on the person's ability, will power and a viable vision. In many a case, making a difference largely means, creating a unique or a never heard of work environment that

is enjoyed and desired by all. Making a difference could also mean setting a benchmark or setting an example before the people that will create motivation and admiration among the general competitiveness of the environment. A leader can largely make a difference by touching the lives of people through his skills, care, empathy and persuasion skills.

- Integrity is a much-required ethical value for a leader. "Many entrepreneurs make the same mistake. When they are tired of delegating, they surround themselves with loyal assistants. They are afraid to put in leadership positions with really smart and successful people" says Howard Schultz, CEO of Starbucks. The story of Howard Schultz is a really intriguing one which highlights the value of integrity to a great extent. Howard Schultz earlier worked at Starbucks which previously belonged to Jerry Baldwin. He contributed a great deal of recipes to the company, but never used them in his own company "Il Giornale" when he moved on. After a year of toiling he finally heard of the Starbucks being sold by Jerry Baldwin and took it over making it into a multi-million business stretched throughout the globe.

- Authenticity and genuineness always stand out among the crowd. A leader is best known for his innovative ideas and breakthroughs. A replica can never stand up to the impression of the original. After JK Rowling, many a souls with novelist aspirations have tried to weave magic out of thin air, but none of them have been as successful as the one narrated by our very own JK Rowling. When a thought is the figment of your own mind, of your own experience, your plans and projects have a stronger foundation to build on. Possibilities would wither even before we have a chance to appreciate them, if we run after replicating castles built by others.

- It takes a good deal of perseverance and commitment to pursue a vision. A leader is termed as a leader because he is deemed capable of achieving a benchmark. Turning around or giving up is never an option for leaders. The Wright Brothers created the first aeroplane in a shabby garage, without giving up. They made the dream of flying, a reality. Not every leader has followers, but for sure, all leaders have opposers ready to oppose him at every step. But leadership isn't about proving someone wrong, it is about proving your worth to yourself. Good leaders lead to avenge evils, not to revenge rebels. A good leader always holds his ground like a mountain on guard.
- Taking a stand in the face of adversity; acting boldly in the face of inclusion and justice stands for courage. Paika Bidroho in 1817 is one of the finest examples of courage, set by Bakshi Jagabandhu, who led the rebellion against the tyrant English monarchs, marking India's very first Struggle for Independence. It takes courage to stand up to your enemies but it takes a lot more deal of it to stand up against your friends. As a leader, it is not always that you will have a hunky-dory relationship with your fellow team members and followers. At times you have to oppose when they deviate.

- Nothing can beat the confidence of a person with knowledge and wisdom. When you know your tools and your ground; you shall reap a fortune. With wisdom even the greatest of devastations can be avoided and prevented. In 1969, Pele, the personification of football was travelling across Nigeria, when it was under severe civil unrest. Such was the influence of the man that a 48-hour ceasefire was agreed upon. It was strange, because the whole country was divided and in conflict, but his presence could really postpone the gore and blood.
- Temperament and transparency of a leader, ensure the team an extra mile of mileage. A leader, who is in control and moderation of his own temperament, is in control of his projects and followers as well. A person who cannot control his own emotions and outbursts will rarely be able to contain the flow of emotions of the many forces around him. If the person in front knows how to affect you, then he is in charge. He can make you do things out of anger and impulse and usually the result of such actions do not favor the doer.

Leadership is a wonderful journey, the way you should not travel, without a ticket, the same way; you should not lead without your values and ethics. Only your values can make this journey from good to great.

11

Leading with Ancient Wisdom

Often Ancient wisdom is tabooed to be boring. However, there is so much to learn from the Ancient stories and scriptures. In fact, lot of new generation leaders have been using the sacred Bhagavad Gita as a true inspiration for the so called – leadership models.

Though topics like Leadership is much talked about in last few decades, the principles of leadership have been demonstrated thousands of years back in Indian, Roman and Greek mythology. One of the greatest examples from Greek mythology was Socrates who believed that wisdom comes from accepting that we don't know much and there is lot to explore.

As we all know Lord Rama was exiled and utilized his exile period to bring about a cultural change through bringing together, tribals and forest dwellers. At that time, his wife Sita, was already captured by the barbaric demon, Ravana. Lord Rama in his search for Sita, came across Sugriva, who was wrongfully denied access to his family and property, and ultimately was banished from the grounds. On hearing this, Lord Rama proposed to help him, but in one condition. The condition was, he would help sugriva, win the crown to the throne by defeating his brother Bali and in return, Sugriva would help Lord Rama with his (Vaanar Sena) Ape army, to rescue Sita from the clutches of Ravana.

It so happened that Ravana was successful in defeating Bali with the help of Lord Rama which made him indebted to him and he being grateful to Lord Rama, willingly allowed his entire army to Accompany him to Lanka, where the demon resided. They moved on foot, to the farthest southern end of the nation, under the leadership of Lord Rama.

On reaching the end, the sea was raging and high tides accompanied with roaring waves were crashing on the coast of now called Kanyakumari. Lord Rama was deep into meditation for two days. Finally, after so much pain and trying different strategies, they got a solution from the God of the seas, Varun, to start the construction of a bridge to reach Lanka. Lord Rama was the initiator of this bridge construction. He initiated with an offering to Lord Shiva and delegated the various activities and responsibilities to experienced architects like Nal and Neel, and inspected every stone before it was laid on the sea. He overlooked the working and the construction of the entire bridge and made sure that the bridge was safe enough for the army to tread by. He then led his entire army to Lanka, all safe and sound and declared war against the demon.

By that time, both the Ape Army and Lord Rama were being ridiculed for trying to build a bridge through the sea. Once the bridge was made, the overconfident tyrant demon, made fun of the Ape Army boasting of his invincibility. But as mythology states, we all know what happened at the very end. Ravana's own brother, Vibhishan helped Lord Rama to defeat Ravana and helped him to rescue Sita.

Ramayana was an epic, of the Vedic ages in India that have provided us with exceptional leadership examples.

- Rama willfully accepted his exile in order to appease an angry step mother, this shows compassion and sacrifice.
- This is also a show of bravery and self-confidence which shows that he was sure of himself that he will be able to survive and fend for himself.
- He is the epitome of humility, though he was the incarnation of Lord Vishnu, all the five elements were under his beck and call. Yet he chose to respect their boundaries and asked for help to the God of seas, Varun to lead him the way.
- Lord Rama has set the bars of leadership through example. He himself was a skilled warrior. He could have asked his younger brother Laxman to assist Sugriva, but he himself took the charge.
- He offered help before he asked for help. This makes for one of the best qualities in a leader.
- He made sure to look after every detail of the Bridge formation, making him a great guide and mentor.
- He led an army of unskilled warriors that needed constant guidance and mentoring and Lord Rama made sure he catered to all their informational needs.
- Lord Rama's generosity and humility lead the Ape Army into making his mission as their own. They fought as one, with the sole purpose of freeing Sita from the demon.

While Ramayana Depicts a leadership style which is more of coaching and mentoring, Mahabharat is the epic that taught people how to be a king maker, rather than becoming a king himself.

Are We Leading?

Days before the Mahabharat would start; Duryodhana went to Lord Krishna, seeking for help. Upon being asked, what he would refer, Duryodhana asked for the vast Yadav Army that would be on his side during the war and fight for him against the Pandavas. The Pandavas on the other hand, were happy to have Lord Krishna and his guidance to take them through the war. This is because Arjun knew what an armed army cannot achieve, can be achieved by an unarmed Krishna. The power of strategy speaks more than words.

Arjun was a highly sensitive but righteous and brave warrior. When on the war field, he faced his teachers and his relatives against him, he refused to pick up his bow and fight.

"In front of me, there stand my relatives, my Guru, whom I have revered and known since my childhood. Seeing them standing against me, with the intentions of war and bloodshed, makes my mouth dry and hair stand on ends. How shall I aim my bow and arrow to my revered Gurus and Godfathers before whom my head should bow with respect? Isn't it against my dharma?"

To this, Lord Krishna replies, "The soul is eternal; it can neither be destroyed nor be created. You will encounter many issues where you have to perform your duty as a warrior first and then of a relative. You should not have compassion for opponents who are not worthy of your feelings and compassion. To wage a righteous war, is your dharma. Be courageous and face the inevitable. Be armed with your bow and charge to perform your duty."

Mahabharata teaches us a lot about modern and present day leadership.

- Lord Krishna was known for his political alliances and his diplomatic strategies which is a must in order to combat against the not so fair world.
- He led the Pandavas from behind the curtains. He never took part in the battle but always gave a piece of his mind with subtle hints for Arjun to figure out the way ahead.
- Lord Krishna never picked up his weapons and never hit anyone, but with his ability and manipulation he could strike down hundreds of enemies.
- He allowed his team to take lead, instead of leading them around or to be precise bossing them around.
- He fought for the right cause and for the common welfare of the Pandavas. Though he used diplomatic means, the agenda was same all through, to fight for what is just.
- He brought out the concept of strategist and implementer, as two different entities.
- He modified the concept of management into strategic management, which was way more efficient and rewarding than the latter.

As compared to olden times, today's youth prefer more of the Leadership that Lord Krishna follows. A style that would let them know the meaning of their jobs and guide them instead of spoon feeding them. Youth of today wants a good guide that would show the way, not carve the path. If there are unskilled people, then leadership of Lord Rama should be preferred where leading by example is followed and suits best for the lot.

12

Emotional Intelligence for Leadership development

Emotional Intelligence (EI) was popularized by Daniel Goleman in his book 'Emotional Intelligence: Why It Can Matter More than IQ' in the mid-90s. Since then this concept has driven nations to think beyond IQ as a measure of intelligence and therefore academic development and success.

Before we move on to how emotional intelligence is important, it is important to understand this concept. There are five main areas in emotional intelligence:

- Understanding of self or self-awareness: being aware of one's own thoughts, feelings and the ability to acknowledge and accept the same.
- Control of emotions: an understanding of emotions comes the ability to control and correctly express one's emotions. This prevents building up of emotional energy and helps one to live life with ease and a sense of emotional balance.
- Self-motivation: ability to acknowledge, accept, express and control emotions bringing in self-motivation and also self-confidence and emotional security.
- Empathy: a person who possesses all the above traits will be easily able to understand other people's emotions as well. This would nurture the quality of empathy- to be sensitive towards others' emotions and feelings.

- Relationship skills: the result of all the above qualities is good relationship building with people around us. Once we are secure with our own emotions, have a fair amount of control and healthy expression, and sensitivity towards others' emotions, we will be able to make people around us comfortable. The result being great emotional bonding and building of healthy relationships.

Once we apply these, we can get an understanding of how important it is to develop these skills. For example, self-awareness can be the key for introspection at an early age, can result in mindfulness and can develop a good vocabulary of emotions. This will help parents and teachers to understand the child better, since the child is himself more self-aware.

Control of emotions and healthy expression is extremely important during teenage, since this is the time for sensation seeking and fight for autonomy. If adolescents are able to express themselves in healthy ways, through sports, arts or anything that does not lead to self-sabotage, it can keep them emotionally secure and would help us to raise confident, mature adults.

Self-motivation is a major issue faced by maximum adolescents and young adults, since their underlying emotional needs have not been met. Hence, they are dependent on motivation from external sources to work hard and achieve. Once self-motivation is inculcated in their personality, they can perform at their peak level and would never lose focus because of adversity in life.

The reason we find many young adults 'cold', 'self-centered' and 'disconnected' is that they have not been sensitized to others' emotions. Lack of empathy can lead to a great sense of emptiness and superficial social connections. Therefore, empathy is a skill that must not be neglected, so that one can share a great bond with others and learn every day skills from a healthy social life.

Finally, relationship skills are mandatory to function well in a more than ever open society. A person cannot thrive and develop completely by neglecting the outside world and the amazing diverse people who have so much to offer to a curious mind.

These five aspects are interdependent and cannot be mutually exclusive as one leads to the other. Hence, all these areas must be well understood to be able to convert this understanding into realization and finally into action.

If as responsible adults, we take the responsibility of developing emotional intelligence in the young, that too at an early age, it would drastically reduce the chance of any mental health concern. Imagine a young generation that knows what it is going through, that can explain how it feels, and that can offer good relationship to others wouldn't this generation be self-supporting? Would they always require a person to depend on the way they do so in the current times? In my opinion, emotional intelligence if taken seriously, can change the emotional energy of the world, and can enable each person to live happily. It is a revolutionary concept.

So, what can be done from our end? As parents, caretakers and teachers, we can include this in education and daily life in several ways:

- Making emotional intelligence mandatory in school

- Using a dictionary of feelings and emotions. Such a vocabulary build would be very useful in understanding and expressing an emotion.
- Using smileys and emoticons to explain emotions to children.
- Teaching the concept of boundaries and privacy to children, so that they learnt to respect others' values, opinions, and culture without personal bias.
- Including related exercises into project works. It could be as simple as writing a diary for oneself, about how the day went and the nature of emotions one could feel.
- Exposing children and adolescents to movies that explain emotions well.
- Including this concept in dramas, plays and different art forms.
- Conducting an 'Emotional Check' once in a while for each child- where one is allowed to talk to the teacher personally and also express one's experiences to the class if he/she wishes, so that it is a learning experience for others as well.

Implementing these ideas could completely transform the quality of education, as academic growth would be enhanced due to a good sense of emotional security. This can equip the young superheroes to discover their strengths and skills, leading to academic and social success. Therefore, emotional intelligence once developed in the early formative years could provide a solid foundation for a healthy future. After all, it is a matter of our young super heroes who would save the world tomorrow!

13

Empowering the young guns

As we grow older and older, we realize how important is Leadership development at an early age. Life would have been a lot more different if we would have got a lot of exposure on how to lead a successful life in more practical ways.

The need of the hour is to discover what exposure and opportunities can be given to children from now on, before their beliefs and personalities have solidified. I am sure most of you can relate to this situation and more so if you are grappling with these questions regarding your child:

Does he or she communicate confidently?

Does he or she interact with you?

Is he or she comfortable in a group of strangers?

Does he or she manage time well?

Does he or she have any stage fear?

Does he or she have enough friends or can he make new friends with ease?

How about listening skills? Is he or she patient while listening?

Does he or she always come up with creative ideas? Does he or she take failure positively?

Does he or she have a role model or someone who is a source of inspiration? (It can be anyone – Mahatma Gandhi, Nelson Mandela, Mother Teresa, Messi, M S Dhoni, Virat

Kohli, Tony Robbins, Deepak Chopra or even one of their Mentors).

If these answers are not favorable, it is a wake-up call. We need to certainly think about what we as parents, teachers or mentors could do to prepare our children for a better future.

Why we need leadership during early age?

Many of us, through exposure to popular media, largely associate leadership with professional adults who are in executive management roles in politics, government, or business. However, if we reflect on our life experiences, we notice that leadership opportunities really begin in youth and this is where the most influential leadership life lessons emerge.

We need to be encouraged, role modelled, and nurtured to develop these skills and it should begin in childhood.

How to create Leadership ambience for children?

- Set a good example: As a leader, you realize the importance of setting a good example for your team.
- Encourage team activities: Early on, identify children's interests and encourage their participation in group activities.
- Handling failure: The best leaders learn to handle failure as gracefully as they handle success. Children need to learn to handle the loss and move forward.
- Build negotiation skills: Every good leader knows the art of compromise. Teach them negotiation skills like never giving up something without

asking for something else in return. Dealing with people needs more than just communication. Negotiation skills are necessary for individualistic growth for survival. The only way is to let them peruse their interests and leave them to develop their own personal relations.
- Hone decision-making abilities: Children should learn how to make good decisions as early in life as possible. Teach children to weigh the pros and cons of each option in order to make the most informed decision possible. This will help them to make correct decisions in everyday life.
- Find a mentor: A trusted friend or family member can be a great mentor, especially if that person is accomplished in an area in which child expresses interest.
- Encourage reading: Develop reading habits, it's a fountain of wisdom. Studies have shown the benefits of reading for fun in childhood, with children who read having greater intellectual progress in a variety of subjects.
- Reward optimistic thinking: Optimism is the key, especially when that optimism is connected to attempting to reach a goal.

How to we infuse leadership?

The best answer to this question is to - Catch them young.

Let's be honest! We all want to see our children being successful. As parents, nothing gives you more joy than looking at your little one being a conqueror. But it's not going to happen by itself. As parents, we need to inculcate in our child's leadership qualities. Here are a few tips as of how to do it:

- Develop public speaking skills

    Studies show that the fear of public speaking is faced by almost eighty-five percent of youngsters. Speaking skills are necessary, good speaking skills are a need. What to do now? Work on their vocabulary and encourage them to speak in front of others. Start small, maybe in front of close friends and then move it to a bigger audience.

- Summer and Winter camps help

    Summer camps usually believe in holistic development. They have trainees usually working in the field of psychology, trained to give your child the mould to find their calling. They also get in touch with peers which help them form bonding among them. It also teaches them to be adjustable.

- Include them in household decision

    We are not talking about giving your child all the control. Do give them the power to take part cohesively in the family discussions. Encourage them to put their points through and consider them as important. This will help them reflect upon their actions and decisions.

- Encourage them to experiment

    Early age is necessary to be kept open for experimentation. The more the child is let free to experiment, they would be inclined more to dabble into places. This will help them to discover their passion and interests.

- Let them ask questions

    No matter how much uncomfortable it makes you, never stop your children from asking questions. The reason? Of course, as parents you know what information is to be fed to the child. There will be days when these sorts of conversations will not result in positive results and might even create conflicts but it will work to create a foundation of trust between you and your child.

- Be strategic

    Dealing with children emotionally might not have the best long-term effect on them. It is better to deal with them strategically. This has two-fold benefits: 1) they would adopt your style of reasoning and 2) the child would look up to you as a reliable figure.

These, in conclusion are the ones I feel are the most important of the things to do to infuse leadership qualities in a child.

14
Sharp minds – Mental health for future leaders

The younger generation is the most valuable asset that we have, as they would be our future leaders who would guide nations and lead to the evolution of the society at large. However, this most valuable asset is fragile, and needs utmost care and attention for overall wellness. The sad part is, their needs are not often recognized.

The youngsters in their growth period need the right kind of education, emotional warmth and intellectual stimulation, so that all of this is conducive to their overall wellbeing. Since they find themselves in a place where they cannot verbalize their needs and experiences, they require us to put up more efforts to bridge this gap. In this process, they may be misunderstood and if not provided with the right kind of guidance, they channelize their frustration through reckless behavior.

If we throw light into the basic needs of young people, we understand that the major need is support. It can be in various ways:

- Support in terms of good education, and opportunities to explore and accomplish.
- Familial support, so that the child learns to form secure attachments and can be a secure adult in the future.
- Support during times of stress, so that one learns to see failure as challenge, and develops a sporty attitude.

- Appropriate guidance when there is tendency to indulge in risky behaviors.

Adolescence is indeed a period of storm and stress. Even children face daily challenges as they learn to interact with their environment and strive to fit in with others in their world. In this process, the youngsters may often fall prey to various kinds of mental health issues.

Statistics around the world report that more than half of our young generation are not correctly guided when it comes to mental health. Symptoms of mental health issues are missed, and this creates a huge amount of stress for them. As adults, it is our duty to educate ourselves in this regard, so that mental health does not go for a toss.

Some major problems that the younger generation faces are lack of attention or concentration, emotional trauma and abuse, peer pressure, bullying, academic pressure, depression and related issues. These could be either a result of inability to cope with adverse situations in life (for example, divorce of parents, death of a family member or a pet, failure in exam, natural disaster, economic failure or financial burden), or a lack of connection or belongingness.

So how would we be able to understand and observe these? Here are some symptoms that children and young adults show that are indicative of underlying problems:

- Social withdrawal
- Sudden change in behavior
- Sudden drop in academic grades
- Change in eating and/or sleeping habits
- Apprehension, or being on the edge
- Creating distraction for others in class

- Drop in health
- Anxiety
- Always being in a state of worry or fear

These symptoms once observed, should be reported to a mental health worker, who can correctly address the issues faced by the child. In order to be observant, there is a need to spread more awareness about mental health in children, so that these problems are not labelled as 'childish behavior' or 'attention seeking behavior' where problems underlying them are deep rooted.

In many nations, there is a concept of mental health champion. A mental health champion is one who engages extensively in workshops and programs for the sole purpose of making people aware, and it is indeed an honorable task. This concept should be adopted by all nations, as no nation is untouched by the scathing state of mental illness in children.

Another great idea is to make mental health a compulsory subject in schools. To introduce the concept to young children, the instructors could make use of plays, skits, videos and involve children in projects. This will not only help them understand the nuances of mental health, but will also remove the stigma around such issues. No parent should feel ashamed to bring their child to a psychologist or a psychiatrist. In fact, they should be respected and appreciated by the society at large, since they are truly contributing to the overall growth and development of the child.

On the other hand, we also observe children who are extremely gifted, and who fall on the extreme side of the bell curve. These children are very delicate, as they need their parents to make more efforts in their upbringing. Such children need more intellectual stimulation, lack of which results in extreme frustration, causing behavioral issues. There are special schools and classes for such children, where their needs are catered, and from where they learn to make a huge difference in the society.

Therefore, looking at the entire scenario from a birds' eye view, we can understand that there are diverse issues that our child could be facing. Ranging from learning disorder to intellectual superiority in terms of academic life, and from attention deficit to depression in emotional health. All we need to do is to be sensitive enough to understand the child's world.

According to me, it is better to enter the child's world and get an understanding of life according to the child, instead of forcing or dragging the child into our 'normal' world, where the child may not be comfortable. It is through this approach that the child would feel understood, supported and connected, and only then would the child open up truly. Unfortunately, we are always too keen to sabotage the child's growth by dismissing certain needs as mundane.

To conclude, I can only say that the young generation is like a pearl in an oyster. We need to discover the true quality of the pearl by polishing it in the right manner, and even more importantly, we need to make the child believe that he has amazing qualities that make him unique in his own way, and that this uniqueness does not have to fit into any terms or conditions. Only then, we can pride ourselves as good parents, teachers or care-takers.

15

Don't just survive, thrive

> IF YOU ALWAYS DO WHAT YOU HAVE ALWAYS DONE
>
> YOU WILL ALWAYS GET WHAT YOU HAVE ALWAYS GOT
>
> – Abraham Maslow

There is a fundamental difference between thriving and surviving. Surviving means, "to continue to live or exist," while thriving can be defined as "growth, prosperity or flourishing".

How come, when so many of us claim to have a goal of thriving, the majority of us are still just surviving?

Signs You're Living in Survival Mode

1. You choose the path of least resistance.
2. You are more reactive than proactive
3. You blame circumstances or others or find excuses when things go wrong.
4. You don't speak your mind because others might disagree.
5. You don't listen to hear. you listen to answer.
6. You see failure as the end result of things.
7. Change scares you.

What would your "great life" look like? Take a few moments to imagine it. Earning money, doing something you love, spending free time doing something you love, being with people you love to hang out and the like.

Imagine it now.

Okay, come back.

Now take a few moments to imagine what your life will be like if you keep living in mediocrity- Continuing with a "boring" job, living an "unsatisfactory" life.

Where will you be in 20 years if you keep living like that?

Now image being on your death bed thinking about your life left behind. How will you feel if you live a life in alignment with your core values?

Do you feel it's meaningful to thrive or you are just blending with the crowd? Is that what you are living for? Being among the crowd?

A great life is when you wake up excited every morning, and go to sleep content every night. A great life is when you know you've done a great job each day, each week and that you're truly living the life you want.

Isn't that worth changing for?

- **HOW TO START THRIVING**

1. **Explore the Things You Love to Do & What Comes Easy to You:**

   Think back on your life, and remember things you wanted to be, the habits you developed naturally, the games you played, the books you read, and see how they may apply to your life and career today. You might be surprised by the connection points that have been right under your nose all along. We are all born with a deep and meaningful purpose that we have to discover. Your purpose is not something you need to make up, it's already there. You have to uncover it in order to create the life you want. You can begin to discover your passion or your purpose by exploring two things:

What do you love to do? And what comes easily to you? Of course, it takes work to develop your talents- even the most gifted musician still has to practice but it should feel natural like rowing downstream rather than upstream.

2. **Ask Yourself What Qualities You Enjoy expressing the most in the World:** First, ask yourself what are the two qualities I most enjoy expressing to the world? For e.g., Love and Joy

   Second, ask yourself what are the two ways I most enjoy expressing these qualities? For e.g., inspiring and empowering people.

3. **Create a Life Purpose Statement:** Take a few moments and write a description of what the world would look like if it were operating perfectly according to you. For e.g., in my perfect world, everybody is pursuing their highest vision where they are doing, being, and having everything they want. Finally, combine all three into one statement, and you will have a clear idea of your purpose.

4. **Follow Your Inner Guidance (What Is Your Heart Telling You?):** Decide where you want to go. All you have to do is decide where you want to go by clarifying your vision, then lock in your destination through **goal setting, affirmations, and visualization**, and then start **taking the actions**

that will move you in the right direction. With every picture you visualize, you're "giving inputs" to reach the destination you want to get to. Every time you express a preference for something, you are expressing an intention. If you don't interrupt the process with a stream of negative thoughts, doubts, and fears, your inner guide will keep unfolding the next step as you continue to move forward.

5. **Passion Test**

    Developed by Chris and Janet Attwood, **The Passion Test** is a simple process. You start by filling in the blank 15 times for the following statement: "When my life is ideal, I am." The word(s) you choose to fill in the blank must be a verb.

    Once you've created 15 statements, you identify the top 5 choices. To do this, you compare statements #1 and #2 to identify which is most important. Take the winner of that comparison and decide whether it's more or less important than statement #3.

    Then take the winner of that comparison, and decide whether it's more or less important than statement #4, and so on until you've identified the passion that is most meaningful to you.

    Repeat the process with the remaining 14 statements to identify your second choice. Then repeat the process until you've pinpointed your **top 5 passions in life.**

6. **Align Your Goals with Your Life Purpose and Passion:** Once you know what your life purpose is,

organize all of your activities around it. Everything you do should be an expression of your purpose. If an activity or goal doesn't fit that formula, don't work on it. You don't need to completely overhaul your life all at once. Instead, just lean into it, bit by bit, and pay attention to the feedback you're receiving from others and in terms of the results you are producing, and also to how you are feeling.

7. **Listen to what other people appreciate about you:** you can find your purpose in what people thank you for. So, keep noticing what people are appreciating in you.

8. **Surround yourself with others who thrive:** When you surround yourself with colleagues and friends who have big ideas and are doing something to make them happen, it motivates you to keep moving towards what you want.

9. **Thrive physically, mentally and emotionally:** Remember to balance your life. Nowadays we are so engrossed in our busy lives that we don't even have the basic needs fulfilled.so Eat well, sleep well, and make time for play. Find at least 1 -2 friends with whom you can share your feelings.

10. **Constantly build yourself:** It is very important that you never forget to be your own best friend and constantly look for ways to build up yourself. Stop neglecting yourself. Give yourself the time you need to do whatever it is you want to do. Read great books that end up building your self-confidence and help you grow as an individual. Give yourself the permission to take that much needed vacation

you have been wanting for so long. Find whatever works for you and stick to a plan. When you learn to be your own best friend you will begin to realize that you absolutely got this and have what it takes.

11. **Celebrate the little wins:** You probably have major long-term goals that you're tackling with. But as you probably know, these huge aspirations won't get accomplished overnight. As "This is a journey—a hard one—and the only way to make it sustainable and bearable is if you actually acknowledge your small successes along the way." By celebrating those tiny wins, you'll find a much-needed daily dose of motivation.

12. **Think you're unstoppable:** When you view yourself as unstoppable and everything as possible, you can stay motivated through both the ups and downs as an entrepreneur. You'll be amazed at the doors that open up when you start believing that you can accomplish anything.

So don't just survive, Keep thriving.

16

Communicate with a difference

Communication is a part of our existence. Defining in simple terms, communication is the imparting or exchanging of information by speaking, writing, or using some other medium. All of us know the basics of this, right? Strike up a conversation, communicate your response and get back a response. This is what we make the basic algorithm of communication.

But let me tell you. Whatever you know about communication is much more and truly amazing. Did you know your way of communication can make and break relations? The way you communicate defines your whole personality and affects your personal and interpersonal relations.

We choose our verbal communication each and every day. We can have a little influence on our words. We choose our words to create the kind of response we want to generate. What we do not have an idea about is actually our non-verbal communication. We will here categorize each type of communication and talk about how to improvise it.

Verbal communication makes way for deeper connections and it can make you seem more approachable. Most people mistake it for the words that they use. Words are important and are directly influential but they do not make you popular or connected to the other person. Then what does it take to make a good conversation? How can you be a good conversationalist? Here are some ways to effectively use verbal communication. Master one tip at a time. It will make you go a long way.

- Be attentive to the speaker. Most of us are not purely into the conversation. We are either half-in or half-out of it. That is just plain disrespectful. If you do not want to engage in a conversation, don't do it but if you do, give the speaker your whole attention. Do not pretend because the speaker will know if you are being genuine or not.
- Assume that you can learn something from the conversation. No matter what the designation and profile of the person, they will always have some information you don't.
- Do not ask straightforward questions. For e.g., if you ask someone, "were you terrified?" the person will only concentrate on the dominant word in the sentence, that is, terrified. They will give you an answer which would be 'yes' or 'no'. This cuts down on the ability of the person to stimulate their brain to think. Instead, use the trick that journalists apply. Ask non-specific, open ended questions. Taking the above example, instead of using "were you terrified?" try to make the question more open-ended. Try asking, "How did that make you feel?" it will make the speaker more comfortable as you are giving him/her appropriate space.
- Always follow up with the last statement. It usually happens that while listening to someone else, we let our mind wander on other things. For example, if someone mentioned eating bagels, our brain associates it with that one time we ate a bagel. We then decide that we would tell this person

about that memory. This will instantly make us subconsciously unconnected to the other person. Instead, follow up with the last sentence that the person has spoken. It's a very subtle trick, but works for you to be seen as understanding.
- If you do not know the answer to a specific situation or question, be honest to the other person. Do not talk about it until and unless you know at least something about the topic. Conversations should not be cheap.
- Never compare yourself with another. Remember that what the other person experiences would be totally different from yours. Experiences and the emotions experienced from it are never the same. Do not try to interpret it either. All you can do is give yourself time. They do not need advices. They just need an ear to hear them, without judgment.
- Do not repeat yourself. You have told the topic once. No one likes rehearsing it. If you do need to do it, keep it crisp and short.
- Similar to repetition, people do not like to have unnecessary information. Cut it out. People are interested to know how you felt or dealt with the situation. They do not want to know the places or people's names.
- If you are given the chance to choose between listening and speaking, choose to listen rather than speak. We have often caught ourselves eager to talk but imagine the frustration of nobody listening to you. It is important to listen rather than speak. People with good speaking skills are actually one of the good listeners as well.

- Last but not the least; listen with the intent to understand and not to reply. This is a very important aspect that most people do not pay attention to.

These were some tips for an effective verbal communication. Verbal communication can never be successful without non-verbal communication. What is that? Non-verbal communication between people is communication through sending and receiving wordless cues.

It includes the use of visual cues such as body language, distance and physical environments/appearance, of voice and of touch. It can also include the use of time and eye contact and the actions of looking while talking and listening, frequency of glances, patterns of fixation, pupil dilation, and blink rate.

Out of these many non-verbal cues, three are the most important.

1. **Posture**

   The posture represents your subconscious approach towards people, if you are open to them or not. Slouching your shoulders and folding your hands over your chest gives the message that you are not confident and that you are not open to other people. You project the need for protecting yourself, emotionally or physically. Instead, try to stand on both your feet putting equal balance on them. Be upright and interact with gestures. It projects confidence and puts the other person at ease for interaction.

2. Speech pattern

If you talk fast and speedily, it triggers the other person that you are either nervous or are holding onto the information. You can judge for yourself. It won't make you sound like a person who knows what they are saying. Try to take your speech slow. Be consistent with words and keep yourself from taking too many short or long pauses. You can follow the other verbal patterns that I wrote above for an effective verbal communication.

3. Eye movement

Always choose to look directly into the person's eye. It establishes that you are genuine and interested in having the conversation. There is an entire language that eyes can communicate. For example, slanted eye contact tells you that the person has taken offence on something or is upset.

Coming down to written communication, cultivate a habit of writing. This will train you with words. Writing e-mails and text message would not fulfil the need. Writing on paper is advisable. Take this advice from poets who tend to prefer writing down to typing on a laptop.

Using the right words is also impactful. A simple word creates different emotions. So, pick and choose your words with caution. E.g., the word 'scared' has less impact than 'terrified'. Writing would only improve with practice so keep your eye open and observe, listen, create- this is the only motto to live by.

Why it's OK to ask questions

Agreement to every statement has been like a tradition to the Indians. People follow rituals and cultures without questioning them. It's so easy for a leader who initiates something new and people follow it blindly. Now, when we are taught not to ask questions, let's see what happens when we ask questions.

Questions related to studies would bring in creativity in children and would do better in exams as they understand the subject better. Sometimes it's like, 'either we understand everything or understand nothing' which is also a reason that we don't ask questions.

Let's take an example of a child between 2-5 years old. The child starts looking at things with utmost curiosity and starts to understand why it is made this way. Though as parents we try to stop them, they wouldn't give up on their curiosity. So, we should be prepared to answer their questions and not stop them from asking questions.

Creativity-Curiosity is the trait of a leader who will not give up easily and move on till the end.

Teachers often scowl at students who ask questions as they expect them to understand and follow what they teach in school. The outcome of this system in school is the increase in the number of coaching centers. If we encourage children to ask questions, they will not fear in putting across their view points. There is nothing called a nonsense or stupid question. It is categorized based on the judgment of individuals. Below is the best evidence that supports the basis of "It's ok to ask questions".

- **Creativity-Curiosity: The best combination for leadership development**

    Leaders have the spark and confidence that they are doing something unique. That uniqueness is the result of being creative. Children are born leaders with these traits. All they need is encouragement and opportunity to showcase their talents, nurture it and applause for their work.

- **Interests- Decisions: Path to Leadership Development**

    By asking questions, Children tend to develop interest towards the subject and might consider a career in it. Though, interests may vary; asking questions will help them take right decisions.

- **Intelligence: Master mind to Leadership Development**

    Intelligence is the only tag that we give our children and pressurize them to study well. Here, studies do require some amount of intelligence. But it does not improve their knowledge and general sense of thinking. By asking questions, it improves the quality of intelligence which in turn shoots up the level of intelligence.

- **Trial & Error as means to Leadership Development**

    When Children do it on their own without any advice, they gain the experience of how to do things right and they learn it quick as they ask questions themselves and find out a way to do it. They learn by asking questions. So, it's Alright!

- **Self-Development: Heart of Leadership Development**

    Sometimes, they ask questions and try to find answers themselves. It's completely okay to ask questions to one- self though it's hard to find answers; it's an important step towards being self-aware.

Now you might ask how to answer their questions. Answer in such a way it doesn't develop fear or hesitation towards asking them questions. Your answers should like a 'food for thought' to them. It should give them an opportunity to probe in more and find out more on the subject. Sometimes, it might be a healthy argument. It's Okay.

So, next time if a child comes and asks you questions, you know exactly how and why you should let them ask more questions. You can also plan for a questionnaire session with them, wherein they will frame questions and you will get to answer them.

'IT'S ALWAYS OKAY TO ASK QUESTIONS' is an important aspect of LEADERSHIP DEVELOPMENT.

17

The path less travelled – Being Creative

Have you created anything new in your life so far? To me that's a definition of being a super leader. The one who has the ability to create new things. It can be an object, a process or a new approach.

Ever wondered how are we able to live life with ease and comfort? Looking at our infrastructure, the information that is available because of the internet, the vehicles that we use on a daily basis to save time, and practically anything around you, like an umbrella or a pen- where have all these come from?

They came into existence because someone dared to ask a question, someone dared to think! And that someone changed lives of many, touched lives and created something that did not exist before, but is now a necessity for all of us.

Unfortunately, in today's era through there is a lot of hype on innovation but the ground reality there is nothing significant happening around us. Things like mobile phones were one of the greatest innovations in recent times but for 7 billion people living in this world there should be more invention and innovation around us.

Creation is the driving force of mankind. If you observe how humans have evolved, you will notice how we have slowly shifted from hunters to gatherers to what we are today. The underlying energy has been a creative force that one cannot get away with. It is this very force that wants us to live better lives, and make life better for others.

This energy is evidently seen in a child. Have you ever seen a child draw something bizarre, that has a name and a function, but which does not exist as an object? I am sure most of us have. And where is that power now? Can we still draw an object so easily? Something that does not exist?

Due to conditioning, lack of stimulation, and many other possible reasons, children forget about this inherent nature. They learn more from text books and less from their own experience, and this makes them think that information is out there in books or on the internet, and cannot possibly be produced from within.

So how can we work with the young generation on these qualities- to create, to imagine and to think out of the box, do exist, although they may be forgotten? Here is where our responsibility lies. We need to create the right environment, use the right language and make it very clear to them that creative thoughts are not random. They cross our mind for reasons of innovation.

Here are some points that are important in accomplishing this goal:

- Help the child be aware. If one can develop a habit of being mindful, one will surely notice surroundings. This improves power of observation.
- Enable the child to be aware of imperfections around him/her. What makes people uncomfortable? Often, smaller problems are indications of major underlying and hidden problems that don't yet have a solution. Encourage questions.

- Equip the child to ask the right questions. Sometimes, it is important to do some ground work before you arrive at a question that is conducive to an innovation. However, all kinds of questions must be entertained while keeping the above principle in mind.
- Make it a practice for the child to regularly take some time off from study/work. All work and no play makes Jack a dull boy indeed! When your brain is consciously not active, it is creating ideas. That's the reason why you are able to answer a question when you were not even consciously thinking about it. This is called insight learning. Most creative ideas occur during this time.
- Help the child to connect ideas. This way learning becomes fun and more neuropath ways are formed in the brain. A brain that can associate different pieces of information together will most successfully be able to generate ideas where one information or one technology can merge with another to innovate something very useful for everyone.
- Get the child to talk to people who inspire, and make him/her feel good. A good self-esteem is necessary to be able to execute creative thoughts and ideas into deeper research and action. Because self-doubt is the biggest obstruction towards discoveries and innovations, create a lot of faith in the child about himself, his ideas and provide your support.
- Use language wisely. Your language should be able to show support, and should focus on the 'do's'

rather than the 'dont's'. For example, instead of saying "Don't be nervous about tomorrow's exam" it would be great to say "I'm sure you will do well tomorrow. I have complete faith in you". This is because the former sentence generates an image and a feeling of nervousness and anxiety, whereas the latter creates a spark of hope and excitement about accomplishing something.

- Monitor how your child treats himself. Does he reprimand or belittle himself following a mistake, or does he take it as an opportunity to learn things differently? If your child can learn to respect and accept himself/herself unconditionally, this sense of security will help the child during tough times.

Therefore, instead of being on 'auto-pilot' mode always, it is always better to consider the alternate possibility of thinking new. Being creative and innovative would not only help with academics or work, but will also generate a different level of enthusiasm in life. There will always be a driving force, failures will be seen as feedbacks, and there will be no stopping- all because the mind is creative, and its basic need is to create.

Imagine how life would have been if we were all on this wavelength! The world would become an exciting laboratory. In fact, it already is, we just need to help the young generation identify objects, concepts, and their own thoughts to experiment with.

18

Community leadership

> "A leader is someone who demonstrates what's possible."
>
> **– Mark Yarnell**

I was quite impressed with Sadhguru's work when he started this movement called Rally of Rivers – a movement to revitalize India's rapidly depleting rivers where millions of people actively participated the cause. A wonderful example of community leadership.

People live in a diverse world characterized by great pressures and responsibilities, changing technology, and challenges in the job market. For any country to succeed we need to empower them to develop their talents and capabilities to become agents of change. One way to prepare them for this is to teach them leadership skills and the best way to get them started is develop on their community leadership skills. The best part about community leadership is there is a purpose and the benefits are directly helpful for the society and that's why many people want to be part of community service.

Let's look at why people don't volunteer:

- They are not really interested in engaging in some work for free unless asked or made mandatory.
- They are so self-absorbed that even if they know how volunteering can change this world for the better, they see it as a waste of time. They would rather let others take the lead. Their ongoing

excuse is that they have enough to deal with in their own lives.
- And then there are those who want to follow the trends. They start volunteering and go all well dressed up on day one, click a lot of pictures and never show up again as they have got enough to show off from day one itself.

What community services give us in return:

- Self-Esteem: The key to lifetime mental health and social happiness is building positive self-esteem. When you can see and quantify the difference you have made, you feel like they can do anything.
- Speaking skills: Through organizing their project, children will have the opportunity to talk to groups about what they are doing (maybe to their church, scout group, school, or civic organizations). If they can begin to get comfortable in front of groups at an early age, the sky is the limit as they get older.
- You can't judge a book by its cover: Many of the assumptions we make about people and the world around us are based on our visual perception, how they look or what they wear. During the food drive, we can witness that many times those who had the least gave the most. People may pull up in nice car and totally ignore the volunteers asking for donations, while someone with tattered clothes would walk over from the bus stop to empty their pockets into the donation jar.
- Emotional Intelligence: Emotions are a difficult thing to read and manage. Because of the interactions with people during the community service projects, we go through a wide range of

emotions, and hence get to learn and manage those emotions real-time.
- The power of action: "That one person can make a difference". No matter how small our action is, it can snowball into something that affects others in a powerful way. The reverberations are beyond those whom they are trying to help. A child working to help others is incredibly inspiring to others, and will ignite a spark in others that can last for a long time.
- Empathy: Working to help others already requires a certain amount of empathy. Going through the process of developing and executing a service project gives children the opportunity to connect with what others are going through on a deeper level.
- Develop Your Soft Skills: You develop authenticity through your daily contact with people. Volunteering gives you a chance to be positive as well. You're doing everything in your power to make society better, and that's the kind of positive attitude that leadership needs. The softer skills of confidence, positivity, authenticity and personal brand are critical to any successful career. Business leaders will inevitably need to use them to gain the trust of their teams, colleagues and professional network.
- Build a Network: The best thing about community work is you get a chance to meet people from many walks of life. Don't be focused on meeting the 'big guys.' See everyone as a contact.
- Be Passionate about Giving: The core principle of volunteering is giving. You help people and groups

to surpass different challenges. You make society better, and that's the kind of passion you need for successful leadership. Choose a cause you're passionate about and maintain the enthusiasm throughout the process of volunteering. Then, extend that mind-set to everything else you do.

- Experiment: Volunteering gives you space for trying new things. This is your chance to take risks and handle different situations differently. When one approach doesn't work, another strategy will. You are only a volunteer, which means you're not getting paid for what you do which means it's easier to take risks and adjust yourself to the situation as your intuition tells you to. That's leadership, right there.
- Leadership development for children through community work: Giving children the opportunity to take on a leadership role in their own community service project helps them put everything together and prepare them for the future. With all of the problems in the world, our future leaders must have a sense of service ingrained in them, to give them the skills and abilities to care for those in need.

Now knowing that community service doesn't just take your time and effort but actually they have so much to give to you. If you start doing it, you can for sure make a change in this world.

Have a great time Volunteering!

Remember, Leaders need power and Power comes to those who are ready to contribute.

19

Leadership development through sports

Nothing beats the feel of fresh early morning air and the soft green grass under your feet to rejuvenate yourself from a tedious week of work. Even the best of workaholics would choose a day in the field over plush office chairs and air-conditioned cabins. As the proverb goes, "A healthy mind resides in a healthy body." Today's corporate world demands the fullest of our talents and potentials. Sports and work space may be from two different realms but they have a lot in common than what seems to the eye. A good sports day can bring in front some of the best leadership traits which can be developed and polished in the work forefront.

One of the most common advantages of being involved in a sport activity is that it ingrains team dynamics in your essence. Leading a group of people certainly has its own benefits and it also instils a sense of social intelligence in the individual. Team work may sound as an easy catch to achieve ginormous targets in real time deadlines, but at the same time it burdens you with the varsity of your team. It takes some real personality weighing skills to assign roles and coordinate the entire team to work towards a common goal. A common problem faced in this case is the conflict between interest and potential of a team member. A good sport in the field can help your team to be knit closer in due course of the game.

A variable response system gets developed in due course of a game being played. In office, the goals needed to be achieved are long term goals and immediate results are rarely the need. In case of a sport being played, the results are almost immediate in nature and at most within 24 hours. The immediate win or loss gives the team a brief of their own dynamics which helps them to better the equation among themselves. There are natural motivators, initiators and supporters in a team and each one of them needs to be responded in a frequency that they can pick up. You do not expect a spinner to be a batsman who can row you through the series, same way you cannot empathize and get your work done where the skills are lacking and mentoring is required. We know there are different leadership styles, but demand of the moment asks the leader to improvise according to the need of the team member at hand.

All good leaders follow a mantra, the mantra of time-management and discipline. As the proverb goes, discipline is the bridge between your goals and your accomplishments. And time management is nothing but self-discipline, self-control and self-evaluation. No sport can be played without discipline and one can never do justice to sportsmanship without time-management. Be it chasing the scores in an ODI or hitting a goal in the 30secs, the ultimate catch lies in the fact, time waits for none. Time is the toughest task master, he who knows to manage and utilize time, is victorious in every field of life. For a leader time is of utmost importance, or else what he and his team strive for, might be no longer achievable or more so taken by someone as excellent a manager who knows his time management skills well.

Success is the end result of small efforts repeated day in and day out. Efforts that are to be put in demand a certain amount of motivation for fueling themselves. A lot of motivation goes into a game by the leader as well as the co-workers. Being a time bound game; it is easy to keep motivation levels high in the team along the entire course of the game. What leaders here, need to pick up is that, in the monotonous corporate, academic or political environment, where goals are long term, motivation factor needs to be upgraded in regular intervals if not in the entire period.

Organizing and strategizing in a sport is the first step towards winning it. If the course of action is undecided, it is very difficult to align your team towards achieving it and it is equally difficult to reach it as each team member would take a different approach and different members would reach the destination at different instances. And it would definitely be an anomaly to team dynamics. Regular participation in sports instils a habit of organizing, planning and strategizing the various approaches towards a given goal. And an added benefit to it is that strategies always have a back-up plan attached to them which no doubt acts as a shock absorber to emergencies and tough situations. These habits are advantageous as well as influential in the occupational forefront where these traits are the most sought after.

Competitiveness is something that runs parallel with the profession, be it sports or corporate. In course of playing against a team there are chances that competitiveness might breed among the team mates as well. It is easy to motivate the team to be competitive against a rival team but extremely difficult to swipe out growing competitiveness among team members arising out of over ambitiousness or insecurities on personal accounts. The team dynamics in any sports team states that "My weakness and his strengths must complement each other to make the team victorious." A subtle leader always knows and understands the line defining ambitions and rivalry and takes necessary steps to avoid such situations. When these topics are addressed in the early stages, the chances of conflict are greatly reduced as well.

One of the greatest lessons learnt on the playground is to accept victory humbly and take failure graciously. A true sportsman always learns lessons from his failures and gains experience from his victories. And most importantly coaches the team from his experiences. Selflessly imparting knowledge and experience leads to a cooperative, closely knit and strong team that trusts, respects and supports you as their leader. They look up to their captain at times of distress, if the captain is in control; they are in control as well. There is no better justification to this than the living embodiments, none other than Mahendra Singh Dhoni. The spirit of leadership of both the level headed leaders is worth a salute.

Talent wins games, but team work and intelligence, conquers championships; and only a good leader can value its importance.

20
What schools don't teach

Let me be honest with you. For almost three decades of my life, I used to criticize my education system. However, when I travelled extensively to other countries, I found that everyone is in a complaining mode about their education system even the developed nations.

Lately I realized so far whatever I have achieved one of the major credits undoubtedly goes to our education system. So why complain and rather start working on bridging the gaps.

When I look back, I felt the flaws in education become more apparent after completion of high school because there was a huge gap in the knowledge gained and its application. It's not easy to change the whole system which makes students lag behind all through their life. So, let's not lose hope and try be more creative in what we can do about it.

1. **Education systems should give more emphasis on analytical skills**

    What can we do?

    - Try engaging them in Brain games like crossword, riddles, Sudoku, scrabble, chess or checkers.
    - Make them join a debate or a reading club. These Groups provide the opportunity to discuss ideas, literature, and problems and possible solutions.

- Help your children build a large knowledge base by reading extensively without focusing on one subject or genre.
- Let them take their own decisions. Give them the space to think about their decisions so that they can weigh the pros and cons of their decisions.
- Encourage them to question. We all know that curiosity makes us smarter. According to Neuroscientist Aracelli Carmago, "The more curious we are about a subject, the more it engages our cognitive functions, such as attention and memory."

2. Lack of personality building practices in our system

What can we do?

- Comparing is wrong, even if you're comparing him to someone who's achieved a lot. Allow your child to express his own personality. Do not limit him to behave in a particular way.
- Every individual has shortcomings, and so does your child. Keep realistic expectations and encourage him to excel at what he's best at.
- 'I want freedom for the full expression of my personality' – had been very rightly quoted by Mahatma Gandhi. Even if others are not voicing the same opinion, teach your child to always make his voice heard.
- And when he speaks up listen to your child's concerns. This will give him a sense of importance and boost his confidence and strength.

- In this developmental stage of life, your child is much more likely to mimic you. Remember that you will need to be on your best behavior at all times. Setting a good example for your child has many benefits.

3. **Education we go through is Irrelevant to Job-Market**

   What can we do?

   - Ask them to read industry news, journals, websites, etc. to learn what jobs are in demand right now. Find out what experts are saying about their industry.
   - Let them attend events, workshops, seminars, conferences and other professional events. These are a great way to stay in touch with current events and issues in any industry. It's also helpful for their networking.
   - Encourage them to take courses and classes. New skills and knowledge can help them do better in their career, and new credentials on their resume can open up new opportunities.

4. **Our system doesn't encourage students to be entrepreneur**

   What can we do?

   Let's remember that it's not just a job which is waiting for ourselves.

   - Teach your child to figure out how problems are temporary. Discuss how to solve a problem with him. Once the skill of problem-solving

Are We Leading?

      is harnessed in your child, he can find out business ideas on the day to day activities.

- Let the child learn from his or her failure. You need to teach your child to try, to take risks. The child should have a positive approach to deal with failures. It was rightly said by someone," Failure is success if we learn from it".
- Be okay with your child taking his decisions. Taking decisions tend to make children responsible and take charge of their actions. It could be as simple as choosing what to eat for dinner or choices of dresses they want to wear. Do not criticize their decisions and allow them to feel good about their decisions and not second guess themselves.

      Allow the child to be unconventional. The times are changing and so are the children. Ask them what they think about a certain practice and how they think it could be better. By doing this you are encouraging your child not to follow rules blindly without knowing the reasons.

- Shower your child with hugs and kisses as an emotionally stable child is going to take failure a lot better and have higher self-confidence. They will know without a shadow of a doubt, they can be and do whatever they've set their mind to. It just takes one person to believe in them, just one.
- Encourage your child to have discussions with an entrepreneur. Meeting a person who has already taken the path they want to take motivates them to move forward consistently.

5. Our system doesn't give hands on experience

What can we do?

- Interning with a company in their career field is a great way to gain hands on experience. An internship can sometimes lead to a job with that company, or at the very least give them experience and references to add to their resume.
- There are many non-profit organizations that have volunteer positions where they can gain work experience.
- Networking is a great way to make professional connections that could lead to a first job.
- Freelancing: Freelancing is a great way to show what they can do. They may have to do their first freelance job for free or low pay just to gain the experience and positive reference. After their first time, however, they now have more experience that they can add to their resume.

6. Too much time on Screen

What can we do?

- Insist that no screens stay in bedrooms overnight. This is a great habit to instill in your children (and into you too!) as it encourages healthy sleep.
- If you encourage your children to put down their phones, then you should put yours down too! Make sure you're modelling healthy behaviors.

- Go on a full-on digital detox of up to a week, making exceptions only for genuinely educational use, given schools often set homework requiring internet research.

MOST IMPORTANT: Don't force your child into something that he's not interested. Just to fulfil your unfinished desires, don't make your child run some unexpected and unwanted races in life which he is not interested in. Instead allow him the freedom to select an activity which he wishes to enjoy and live fully.

21

Parental Leadership

Children learn to lead by watching you.

As they say, "Children grow up by watching their parents and family"; it's essential to spend quality time each day so that there will be connection between children and parents. Sometimes it's very difficult to manage children, home and work. We fail to talk and pay attention to them. That's when children lose co-operation and will not respect you. However, to make you stay close to your children and spend some productive time with them we have the below pointers which will give you an idea of how you can be together apart from their daily routine of school and studies.

- Let them pick a leisure activity (watching TV, eating snack, etc.) of their choice by adding an expectation of study or homework attached to it.
- Encourage creative activities and allow them to include them in their play.
- Be flexible with their choices and preferences.
- Acknowledge efforts and spend some time reviewing their work.
- Plan a fun activity and involve in their play.
- Watch their favorite shows and talk about it.
- Keep calm and listen to their interests.
- Make a to-do-list and share it with your child. They will understand your priorities and will also respect you and you can make that time for something else.

- Encourage them to pursue a hobby/ sports of their choice and show your involvement by showing your interest and making them attend the classes regularly.
- Make plans to spend some quality time together like family dinner time, talking about the day, sharing experiences on a daily basis.
- Involve your children to learn something new. Spend some time teaching them about behavior, etiquette or something that interests them. They will love it.
- Make a rule so that they would know that you are giving them attention and affection. Make sure they follow them and acknowledge them by giving them few privileges.
- Help them in studies, projects instead of sending them to tuitions. They would love to study with you.
- Plan activities to help them understand and remember their curriculum.
- Help them stick to their routine and reward them when they deserve.
- Let them make their planner, which will increase their productivity.
- Make home a place for hangout.
- Schedule activities like planning an outing/ play games with them as often as you can.
- Identify their potential and guide them to pursue what interests them.
- Involve them in decision-making, giving suggestions and ideas.
- Allow them to do something for you.

You can come up with many ideas with reference to the above recommendations. You may use these to see changes in your life and your family relationship. Children need their life apart from pressure of studies and scoring good marks. You, as parents can go an extra mile to give them a loving fun-family-study life. Parents who are struggling for time, just try to give 15 to 30 minutes per day of undivided attention to your children and you will see a huge difference in the way you are experiencing parenthood.

Peers Vs. Parents

I overheard the following conversation from two fifteen-year-old in a bus:

"So, did you tell your mom about going to the party tonight?"

The other teenager, all wide-eyed and worried "Of course not! My mom is not as cool as your mom."

"So, what are you going to tell her?" the other girl asked.

"I'll just make up a story. I'll tell that I'm going to have a sleepover at Tina's place and then just go to the party." she said.

"Does Tina know about this?" the other girl.

"Of course, she does. She is my best friend. She convinced her parents for the sleepover as well." She smiled.

Rings a familiar bell? We all must have lied to our parents about something or the other because they won't 'understand' us. That could have dragged us down to lying to them to escape. There are certain things we just cannot tell our parents. Can we?

So, the question now arises. When did we start equating our peers our secret keepers rather than our parents? Is anything wrong with doing it? Can parents ever be equal to peers? Are you comfortable telling our parents everything?

Let's be honest for a moment. We have all pondered on these questions one time or the other. Why are we making you ponder more on this? Because you need to be fully aware of this to have the ultimate progress in your life.

We utterly depend on our parents for a myriad of basic needs, including love and respect. Adult child relationships can be broken down to the parenting style that is being followed by the guardian. We have the authoritarian parents, the authoritative parents, the ignorant, the permissive and the neglectful parents.

- Authoritarian parents: These are the 'strict' parents. They are demanding of their child but are not effective in fulfilling the demands of their child (especially emotional). E.g., we have all had that one friend whose parents are much stricter than most of them. There is a good chance that his/her parents are authoritarian.
- Authoritative parents: probably known as the most effective way of parenting. These parents are demanding but also reciprocate the emotional and other needs of their children. Could be labelled as the 'cool' parent(s).
- Permissive parents: we all know parents that place huge authority in the hands of their children. The scenario is that the children have more power in the house than anyone else. They are fulfilling of the child's demand but they do not present any expectations and demands from their side.

- Neglectful parents: these parents are simply neglectful. This is the most despised sort of parenting from psychologists all over the world. They neither make any demands nor communicate any expectations to the children. This could spring from several factors such as being too ambitious or irresponsible or several other factors.

Sounds bad, doesn't it? Despite popular belief, most children share a strong bond with their parents and are able to keep that for a lifetime. There are conflicts, of course, but they are able to pull through with understanding. That is where the peers come in the picture. We feel more comfortable sharing certain information with our peers rather than our parents because we have a common understanding that it would be inappropriate for us to share. From where do we come to realize? Well, our peers.

It is not surprising that if we hear one of our peers getting scolded for doing something wrong, we tend to avoid telling it to our parents in the future. In the context of Indian parents, there are a lot of taboo concerned around the topics of sexuality, relationships etc. Thus, we do what our peers tend to do. And we just aren't the only people doing that. Even adults tend to do what their close peers do.

The involvement of parents is the most crucial during adolescence. During the teenage years, it's the friends that take the front seat in terms of influence. This was a huge part of the nature-nurture controversy, before Judith Rich Harris came up with the theory of peers influencing the teenage years. Now do you understand that if you are an approaching teenager, why do you tend to take the word of your peers more?

We all make choices, including children, teens and adults. Their decisions are not just made according to their personalities but on an incredibly complex myriad of factors of which they are not conscious. It is the increasing or decreasing influence depending upon our personal agreement that we tend to act upon it.

How do we strike a balance because clearly, giving more authority of either one in our life could create problems? Here are some hacks:

- Don't get influenced by the thought of falsehood. Peers are not always right, neither are parents. In the end, fall back on your conscience to fulfil your needs.
- Before putting on the blame, look what you have to take responsibility of.
- Make sure you establish a friendly connection with your parents from your side. It would be especially problematic if you have authoritarian parents but it is always good to keep things clear from your side.
- Acknowledge the fact that you, including your peers lack in experience so if you are facing a problem that would need advice from them, do not hesitate.
- Remember, your parents are ultimately guided by the principle to help you. Be as transparent to them as you can.
- If you are being told to make drastic change in your personality, do examine yourself once before proclaiming that the claims are ridiculous.

- Maintain a healthy lifestyle. It has positive influences most people do not understand. It will keep your mood and mind in positive light, making you capable of taking rational decisions.

Lastly, it is alright to make mistakes as long as it does not land anyone in trouble. Always apologize when you are wrong and strive to be your best way possible. There always is a way if you are willing to do something.

Are You A Helicopter Parent?

Do you still have a sore back from running around following your 10-year-old in the playground?

Does your kitchen have a weigh scale to balance your munch kin's nutrition?

Do you have several sleep breaks at night to check on your children whilst they are asleep?

Do you prefer the visiting friends of your child to interact in our presence?

How often do you punch in the unlock pattern of your children's' cell phones?

When was the last time you allowed your child to visit his friends place? More than a month?

Does a fifteen-minute delay of the child, in returning home lead to a string of phone calls and a host of spies?

Do you know who your child sits with, in the class?

Do you prefer to solve disputes and misunderstandings between your child and his friends in school?

Do you still tie their shoelaces?

If you get 5 or 6 questions as yes, my dear fellow parents you have to think again. Breathing down their necks will only give you neck sprains and air locks.

"Wise parents prepare their children to get along without them." The term "helicopter parent" was used in a book by Dr. Haim Ginott named "Parents and Teenagers" where the teens had commented that their parents used to hover over them like helicopters. This term gained popularity and even got listed in the oxford dictionary in 2011.

It's one thing to be protective of your child, and other being over protective to the point of stifling them to frustration and dependence. In order to shape an individual, it takes real life experiences, head on challenges and a fair share of mistakes. If you do not let them spread their wings on ground around you, they will never be able to soar above the clouds.

Me as a child, was always accompanied by my parents to and from school, even though I learnt how to ride a cycle, even got a two-wheeler learners license. My teachers used to keep a five-minute slot for my parents, twice every week, which would comprise of going around enquiring of my weekly progress, though I was the topper of my class. These habits were so infectious that by the end of my 6th grade there were almost 50% of the parents of my classmates who started imitating and following my mother's parenting handbook, ticking off checklists every week, practically raising hybrid babies in grade 7. This not only led to a constricted friends circle during my school days but I was already being called a pet Chihuahua. I still don't have many friends from school and till date I have a very small circle of friends and acquaintances. Some practices do have long term effects.

There was one incident where I distinctly remember, it was during my college days, when a long-lost school friend came to visit me at my home. I could distinctly make out that my mother had checked on us at every 10 minutes interval making sure what we were talking about, though she never intervened. We chatted for about an hour when it was time for him to leave, and we decided to pose for a selfie. It was then that my mother actually came barging into the room asking me to come to the bedroom for a second. I excused myself from my friend and went to her. I could literally see her frantically pacing across the length of the room. No sooner did I enter my room, I was bombarded with questions like, "Which friend is this? I don't remember any such friend from school."; "Why were you taking selfies with him? Is it safe? Don't you think he would misuse the picture?" it took me another 10 minutes of explanations and persuasion, to placate her. And if you want to know if we took the selfie, then yes, I was successful in the mission. Period.

Being a helicopter parent not only does tax you but also taxes your children. Knowingly or unknowingly you start regulating their friends circle, their time table and sometimes even the subjects that they are going to select for their boards. Let them roam free, let them make new friends, let them make their own decisions, let them commit mistakes only then will they know the difference between good and bad. Let them face the consequences of a mistake, let them learn from it. You won't be there every time to shield from the vagaries of the world. Let them chose their friends, do not regulate or restrict the flow of companionship, sure enough as a parent you can give your opinion about a certain someone in the friend circle, but let them make the decision. You can lay flowers beneath their feet on the ground they walk for all you want, but that really doesn't mean that the world doesn't have thorns. Let them know and experience what a thorn is, only then will they learn to value the flowers. Do not fight their battles, let them stand up for themselves and fight of their own.

Stop spying behind your children and most urgently dissolve the spy network you have created to look out for your child in the form of neighbors or relatives. This makes the child a laughing stock as well as a dead target on the tracks. The more you hover around, the lesser freedom your child has, the more restricted his friend circle becomes, the more reserved his nature turns and most importantly he becomes dependent on you. This could seriously affect your child's decision taking skills and it would be a curse for both the parent and child in the long run. Your children might be used to you hovering around them, but other children and their friends aren't used to that. Exhibiting such tendencies before their friends will make you the unpopular parent of the group. The consequences of this may be that your child becomes the loner of the class as the comrades do not want the hovering baggage that accompanies with your child. This might sometimes as well be embarrassing and your child yourself might stop socializing.

Go easy on your child.

- Let them go on trips, drives or birthdays once in a while (without the spies and phone calls of course).
- Do not regulate friend circle, give opinions instead.

- Do not fret and employ spies in 15 -20 minutes delay.
- Stop checking on them on every 5 minutes. Stop taking account of their every second. Give them some "ME" time, it is very much essential to develop a unique personality of their own.
- Stop choosing their subjects for them.
- Do not accompany them to interviews and examinations; let them face it by themselves.

Use the time to enhance yourself, as a better human being. Let go of the worries. Instead of running around them, take rest. Don't be as hard and harsh on yourself as a parent. Live and let live. Instead of hovering, find ways to equip your child with parachutes, so that it becomes a combined effort; your values and their practice. Parenting is a responsibility not a burden, don't complicate it.

22

The futuristic teacher

One thing is pretty clear that if you have to create more leaders, we need to create more teachers and more than a teacher a futuristic teacher who is more forward looking and a teacher who is constantly finding out new ways to teach.

When you ask a child what do you want to become when you grow up how rare is the answer that I want to become a teacher? With time this profession has lost its glory and respect. In earlier times teachers were like God to children and they were their mentors, leaders and a source of guidance for life. So, what changed? It's the environment and not just the education system. Requirement of today's children are way different than the children of previous generations as new concerns have emerged like Teen pregnancy, drug abuse, cyber bullying etc.

So, we all need to move teaching profession from just being a teacher to a futuristic teacher. The teacher who is made for these times is the one who

1. Knows the importance of analytical skills so from the start he tries to engage children in brain games like crossword, riddles, Sudoku, scrabble, chess or checkers.

2. Encourages children to join a debate or reading club. As these groups provide the opportunity to discuss ideas, literature and problems, that's how children open their mind to the world

3. Helps children to build a large knowledge base by reading extensively. And he needn't just focus on one subject or genre.
4. Encourages them to ask questions. Sameer says, 'Did you know that curiosity makes us smarter?' According to Neuroscientist Aracelli Carmago, "The more curious we are about a subject, the more it engages our cognitive functions, such as attention and memory."
5. Knows comparing is wrong. He allows every child to express his own personality. Even if others are not voicing the same opinion, he teaches children to always make their voice heard.
6. Cares about student's health so he tells about the healthy food choices and how essential it is to exercise daily and starts his class by a 5 min meditation session.
7. Keeps realistic expectations from children and encourages them to excel at what they're best at.
8. Remembers that he needs to be on his best behavior at all times. Models how to treat others with kindness and respect. By this he is setting a good example for children.
9. Encourages them to attend events, workshops, seminars, conferences, other professional events, courses and classes which can help children to identify the career of their dreams.
10. Tells them about the disadvantages of spending way more time on screens. He always gives them assignment based on machinery or nature so that they go out, understand and present, not just copy paste.

Are We Leading?

11. Teaches the children about every culture with respect and makes the child understand and respect all of them without any bias.
12. Provides children with weapons against peer pressure. Talks with them about what a good friend is and isn't.
13. Help children understand bullying. Talks about what bullying is and how to stand up to it safely. Tell children bullying is unacceptable. Makes sure children know how to get help.
14. At every parent teacher meet tells parents how to strike the right balance, between their expectations and their child's dreams.
15. Is grounded in reality. He gives options to save money on education to parents such as dual enrolment, better housing options, buying second hand textbooks, selling books back online, earning money while in school, getting a part-time job or working during summers vacation and applying for scholarships.
16. Knows the body image issues and compliments on child's look and allows them to try new looks and styles and also makes sure teens are kept active every day.
17. Asks them to read industry news, journals, websites, etc. to learn what jobs are in demand right now in their chosen field.
18. Encourages children to have discussions with an entrepreneur because Meeting a person who has already taken the path they want to take, motivates them to move forward consistently.

19. Encourages them to opt for volunteering, interning and freelancing before the time for their first interview comes as he knows theory can never beat practical knowledge.
20. Helps the children to create their network in the field of their choice.
21. Tells children to how to balance work life and health with play time so that they lead a balanced and fulfilling life.
22. Most of all he listens more and never forces a child into something that he's not interested.
23. Interacts with the teens positively, increases his involvement in positive activities, is aware of teen's social environment and communicates regularly with their parents. Talks with teen about his concerns, asks him directly about suicidal thoughts. Explain the value of therapy and medication to manage symptoms.
24. Tells them that they should have a frank discussion with their roommate(s) from the very first day of college so as to not make the environment sour.
25. Most of the time, talking about the problems and maintaining a healthy lifestyle can prevent the onset of depression. So, he doesn't brush away their feelings as that can make things worse.
26. Disciplines children through non-violent means. Provide stories, books, movies, etc. that place a high value on treating others with tolerance and respect. Create a culture of respect in the classroom. Encourages them to speak out against violence and injustice.

27. Encourages healthy eating habits. Talks to teen about his eating habits and self-image. Stays emotionally connected with them in a supportive and loving way. Promote a healthy body image. Helps child with self-esteem by respecting his accomplishments that are not related to body weight.
28. Makes child aware that they have a choice as to whether they participate in casual sexual encounters or not. Reminds the child that not only do they have the choice about whether to participate in non-intimate casual sex but that each choice that is made has its own physiological, emotional and relational consequences.

So, it's an appeal to all the teachers who think that teaching is at its dead end to review it. It is not. Also, it's where it is because it didn't adapt with time. If you want the profession of teaching to be alive, glorious and respectful once again it is high time to upgrade. Be a Futuristic Teacher.

Having said it all what the futuristic teacher would need a lot of support from the society, parents and the educational institutions is also sought which keeps them motivated.

Though compensation is the Number one issue for teachers, organizations and parents can do a lot more to give back the same respect teachers used to have some time back.

I would probably like to see something like 'Teacher of the month' award recognized in annual meets.

Most often teachers ask me to suggest a few easy techniques for leadership development and behavioral changes. Based on my life coaching experience I would like to pen down a few. Mostly these are NLP techniques.

NLP stands for Neuro Linguistic Programming. It's the study of successful behaviors and implementation of this study to produce techniques and a way of life that ultimately result in the desired, successful pattern of life. It combines human behavior and language with the knowledge of how brain functions, and uses this to produce excellent methods that can create life changing experiences.

So, these techniques are for all those who are light bearers in the society.

'Light bearers' are those whose roles and responsibilities revolve around guiding others in need, and it is not wrong to assume that teachers, parents, educators and all those who are engaged in upbringing and motivating the future generation are the ones who can carry the light and shine it upon the younger generation.

Neuro Linguistic Programming, if correctly explained, is not just a set of techniques, but rather a way of life. It involves the use of correct language so that the brain and the unconscious mind can cooperate with the conscious desires and bring them into reality. Therefore, this skill set, if applied by the light bearers, can greatly help the young generation to achieve their highest potential.

Although we have all tried our best to bring up children and teenagers as confident, responsible adults, there are places with gaps, and NLP can greatly contribute in bridging this blinding gap.

Considering the young generation, that is faced with problems like a short attention span, addiction to digital devices, peer pressure and a cold attitude towards their care takers and the elderly, parents and teachers cannot help but get into a personal conflict. However, it is always beneficial to remind ourselves of the fact that upbringing is not just parenting, it is also a result of social situations. The NLP presupposition "Everyone makes the best decision for themselves, at a particular time and situation" falls true for both light bearers and youngsters. We may have not always be correct but we try our best. Similarly, the young generation has tried its best, and due to conflicts and influences that still exist, they are faced with problems that we think need to be reprimanded.

Language is the most taken for granted mode of communication. If we can learn to use it wisely, it can create wonders. We can talk in a language that sounds positive, non-judgmental, accepting and inspiring to create a better rapport with youngsters. Here are a few points that deserve mention:

- It is better to focus on what is to be done rather than what is not to be done- the subconscious cannot process negatives (like no, don't, even words like lose), and focus is therefore on the wrong side.

  So, when we say "don't waste too much time on your smartphone", we are creating an image of usage of smartphone, which obviously persists as behavior, and is difficult to get rid of.

  Rather, if we could switch to "You have such a bright mind it would be amazing if you could spend only 2 hours every day in your study." This creates pictures of peaceful study and perhaps the rewards that follow. This inspires the child to produce this behavior and also helps to create a positive relationship with the care taker.

- Much importance should be given to the goal instead of barriers on the path. If you could help your child to clearly visualize the goal, and engage all the five senses in this experience, a new neural pathway is created which helps to engage in behaviors that lead to achievement of the goal. For this, the light bearers need to closely examine their own language.

For example- when a child desires to do well in Math, you can ask the child to imagine what it would be like to have done so well (visual), hear the sounds of other people praising and appreciating the child, and the sound of one's own thought about this achievement (auditory), along with getting in touch with the emotion of joy and accomplishment (kinesthetic). Once this scenario is fixed in the mind, the very thought of studying would produce this image and would inspire the child to move towards the goal.

- When it comes to the child's use of language, be it internal (thoughts) or external (communication), it can be corrected to produce healthy patterns.

For example, when the child is nervous, mostly likely thoughts are "Can I do this?", "I'm not good enough", or something similar. Instead, the child should be encouraged to practice saying "I will do my best", "I'm great at this" or "The universe supports me completely in what I do". This practice can completely change the attitude of the child and can generate a lot of confidence and self-esteem. Can you think of the images that would come to the mind in the former and latter cases?

- Coming back to engaging the five senses the youngsters can be taught to use their senses in all their experiences. This will greatly enhance their power of observation and will result in mindfulness. This practice has far-fetched benefits than we can think of- being present in the here and now, paying attention to detail, being grounded in current reality, and an enhanced attention span along with thirst for more knowledge. Don't you think this can do so much to generate curiosity and feed intellectually?

- It is always easy to blame the younger generation for being aloof from their elders and the family as a whole. However, what we should really ponder upon is- what makes them attracted so much to the other side. Acceptance is something that youngsters experience with their own circles, and any lack of acceptance or gap in communication can result in rebellious teenagers who can be difficult to deal with.

  Therefore, it should be made a practice to express- in gestures and verbally, one's acceptance and love towards the child. Both are equally important. It should also be kept in mind that the two should never contradict because it creates confusion in the child's mind which will keep him aloof from you.

This practice will also help the child to open up and discuss about existing problems or achievements. The result? An amazing bond with the child!

The last of the key things you need to do is to find out the learning style of your child. NLP defines it as VAK (Visual, Auditory, Kinesthetic)

This is just a glimpse of how NLP can help the light bearers to guide the youngsters towards a brighter future. The light bearers have a lot of experience and wisdom, along with responsibility, hence they deserve to learn the best ways to spread love, light and happiness.

23

Are there enough opportunities

A negative thinker sees difficulty in every opportunity. A positive thinker sees opportunity in every difficulty. Opportunities don't happen, you create them. At times we usually see that adversities mar our chances at success and often create hindrances towards our goals. What we fail to understand is that, these are opportunities that pose as adversities to test our limits and perseverance. It solely depends on us as to how we look at a situation and what is our attitude towards it. As the old adage goes, always shoot for the moon, even if you do not hit, you will at least land among the stars.

Belonging to a typical Indian family, almost all of us were raised, listening to various tales that would teach us moral values and ways of life. One such tale has been vividly etched in my mind. A long time ago, in a faraway kingdom, there lived a king who did all that he could do for his subjects, yet he couldn't see his subjects flourishing any further. He used to make rounds around the kingdom, in disguise and often found his subjects, complaining of the various shortfalls of resources that were scarce and the kingdom was unable to provide for in plenty. He decided to test the people of his kingdom. One night he ordered his soldiers to block the main road of the town with a large stone that would hinder the passage of incoming and outgoing carts and travelers. The next day, there was a cacophony in the main market, regarding the large stone. The subjects started complaining how the king and his officials have been neglectful in maintaining the cities and how the king no longer deserved that position. Much was said and debated but none of them made any move to clear out the stone. A few days passed by and the town started to face a setback in trade and commerce as well as a decline in rations. A poor stone mason lived in the periphery of the kingdom, who could barely make his ends meet. He heard about the large stone that was creating troubles for the township. He went to see for himself if it was true and indeed, he found the large stone resting on the very middle of the road. After inspecting it he found that the stone was porous and with the help of a few men, it could be easily removed, but no one bothered, as they were frightened by the sheer size of it and indifferent to the needs of the town. The stone mason finally decided to work it in his own way as to no one was going to help him, either to remove the stone or to help the people.

The next day he started early and reached the place. He started off with chipping the stone and worked relentlessly just pausing for short water breaks. People came and went, some encouraged, maximum ridiculed, but he kept working. By day break, he had cracked open the rock and had started carving out a deity out of it. He worked and worked, until the sun went down. And returned home leaving his project to return the next day and resume. This went on for a couple of more days and the people of the town had stopped paying attention towards him, apart from the occasional taunts and scowls but he paid no heed to them. What he didn't know was that a pair of brown irises was observing him from a far corner. He finally made a beautiful deity out of that block of stone and used his makeshift cart to remove it from the middle of the road. What he wasn't expecting was that, a big pouch was hidden under the once huge rock. He picked up the pouch to find it filled with gold coins to the brim. The king was observing him from a distance and he summoned him the very next day, rewarding and felicitating him with an award, and the position of the royal mason in his palace as he was very impressed as to how he turned a rock into a work of art, at the same time, selflessly helping the city out of its misery.

Folklore and tales are a long line of tradition in families, but when these morals of the folklores are put to use, they work wonders. I have myself seen such incidents where people have created opportunities for themselves, where they indeed had slim scope or had no interest at all.

The hall was filled with aspirants, ready to be absorbed into the company for placement. He never wanted to come in the first place, not for the interview, not for the placement but he sure did want to make himself visible among them. Being seated randomly, one among the crowd; he made himself ready to face the pre placement talk. He just wanted to see where this would take him. An hour wouldn't cost much; he had to take his chances. The talk started with the placement coordinator introducing the company HR and the interviewers. The interviewer was one of the board of directors of the company and he was looking for something that was a bit different from the general crowd. After the generic talk and introduction, he threw a general question to the crowd, "Apart from making money and toiling hard to earn a day's worth, why do you want to work?"

A few people spoke up, saying how they would love to work for the company to gain fame and recognition, while some people stated their passion towards work and how it made them feel alive and kicking. None of which seemed to intrigue them that much. The guy rose up from his seat, seeking permission to speak. And thus, he started,

"I want to work for my country, and I want to work for my nation. I want to work for the upliftment of the country's economy. I want to contribute to the employment opportunities and I want to make national products, a national priority, through quality and cost assurance. I have studied and applied my engineering skills and knowledge in producing quality equipment's in a very cost-effective way and I am currently working on up scaling my small-scale production unit. Not only will it help us to compete with the ever-dominant international cheap replica market, but also create a base economy of ours, that is much less dependent on exports. I want to work for myself, my country as well as for the country that is yet to come. I strongly believe that small steps of patriotism will lead to a huge leap of development in the nation. The basic purpose of our education ministry is to create a brain force capable enough to support and lead the country and I want to serve my nation for the purpose for which it has nurtured me."

By the time he ended, he was given a huge round of applause along with a standing ovation from the recruiters themselves. He was ready to be hired even without an interview but he refused, saying his own company needed him more. To this the recruiters were so impressed that, they awarded him a fund cheque of 300,000 rupees to help him upscale his business along with the offer of partnering with them in future. I had never seen someone turn the tables, so quick, even without having a prior intention of doing so.

From the above stories, we can conclude a few points,

Never let adversities dictate your attitude towards a problem. Work towards it, you never know it might be an opportunity in disguise.

Always try to make the best out of the situation like the stone mason. Never miss an opportunity to show your skills. Instead of breaking the stone or moving it haphazardly, he chose to carve it and then move it. It served two purposes. One, he moved the stone and two; he grabbed the opportunity to showcase his skills which landed him a royal position.

You create your own opportunities. The guy had no intention to sit for the placement and even after being offered he rejected. But he created his opportunity through his voice and communication and landed a good fund as well as a future promise of partnership.

Never miss an opportunity to prove yourself. You might not land on the moon, but the stars will do for now.

Opportunities need to be grabbed, unraveled and created. Nothing in this competitive world is served on a silver plate and offered to you.

There is a plethora of opportunities waiting out there, the only thing is, and one has to keep a keen eye. If the opportunity comes in a disguise, unravel it; if it flashes itself to you, grab it and if it doesn't show up you just create it. There are enough opportunities the only need is to recognize its form.

24

Essential Soft skills for Leaders

Most of the time our ability to do more is restricted due to lack of soft skills even though we are the best when it comes to technical competency. With competition getting stronger day by day the need for soft skills are being felt by everyone irrespective of the industry and the role.

Time and again it's proven that soft skills are very instrumental for personality development from a young age.

Often during my corporate experience, when we were called for town hall meetings mostly on organization wide updates, I used to take least interest in those presentations. I remember number of occasions where I used to fall asleep during those meetings. I could hardly get what the leaders used to talk about. I could not simply connect to some of the leaders due to lack of their speaking and presentation skills.

During the initial days of my career I constantly struggled when it came to present or sell something, the ability to communicate effectively and be assertive but somehow with lot of effort and guidance I could improve my skills.

However, I wish I could have got exposed to soft skills at a very young age.

Though academic learning is usually in the spotlight in schools, but teaching students "soft" skills like self-control and social skills is critical for their success in life, their future career pursuits and overall leadership development which will make them make more valuable for college admissions and eventually for the employers.

Time and again, recruiters tell us they need new hires to have soft skills, an ability to communicate, work well with diverse teams spanning the globe, enhance their communication, teamwork skills, inter-personal relationships, and self-awareness.

Based on my experience we should give a lot of importance to the soft skills mentioned below when it comes to children.

- **Social skills:** Once one of my neighbors came to my home and my son opened the door. My son realized that I was in the kitchen doing some work. He suddenly came to me running and asked me to come and see my neighbor. When I came to the main door, I realized that he has not even asked my neighbor to be seated. For some reason he was not so comfortable talking to my neighbor though he knows my neighbour since many years. I realized as Parents we need to work on him to improve on his social skills.
- **Collaboration:** Nowadays most of the children are on their own. They hardly talk or interact and often believe in individual heroics. Collaborating with others mostly facilitate thoughtful ideas in teams, divergent thinking, group values and encourages team members to push the barriers.So somehow we need to encourage our children for more team work, it might be a sport or might be a gathering.

- **Respect:** Listen to opinions of others, demonstrate kindness. Relationships just break due to lack of mutual respect. There has to be respect for others time and efforts.
- **Empathy:** Empathy is what makes us aware of the feelings of others and when you're empathic you're much less likely to hurt someone else's feelings. Even the use of these simple magical words: 'Thank you, I am sorry, I care for you, I am grateful' can create a huge difference.
- **Managing Time:** Undoubtedly there are too many attractions nowadays and children find it very difficult to manage time and why just children we all find it very difficult to manage time. we must learn different ways of planning and prioritizing our work. One great way to accomplish more in less time is by attaching one positive feeling to each of the task you want to complete.
- **Tenacity:** Where there is passion and ability, a child may deeply explore a project or subject, but they may also become frustrated and disinterested if a new skill does not come as easy to them as they expect. Same applies to adults as well. Learning to stay motivated beyond a specific time, throughout the tenure of a project is an essential skill.
- **Resilience:** Failure must be encouraged to facilitate progress, but progress must be steered toward precision. A new way of looking at things needs to be encouraged, staying engaged with a project and exploring options that were not initially intended. Inaction is unacceptable — for it leads to zero progress. As a Coach On several occasions I

force failure into a project, so that participants may learn to recover, correct course and keep moving forward.

- **The importance of a Plan B:** Always prepare for your first plan, attempt, or trial to fail. Failure is the norm, not the exception, so planning for a glitch also helps to build resilience and maintain motivation. There is no failure in life, Its only a feedback that you need to improve.
- **Anticipating other's needs:** This is critical for high functioning teamwork (as well as being a cool human). I tell my students, "If your parents are throwing a party, take it upon yourself to take care of guests and ask them if they'd like a refreshment," or "don't wait for dad or mom to ask you to start bringing dishes to the dish washer after dinner.
- **Active listening:** To understand the objective, to be clear on instructions and guidelines, to hear inputs and ideas from your peers. Convey understanding by repeating back what you've heard — message received!
- **How to set-up and clean-up:** we all have seen what the Japanese football team did in the 2018 FIFA cup in Russia. After their heartbreaking loss and being eliminated from the world cup the entire team cleaned up their locker rooms and left behind a thank you note.
- **Importance of Preparation:** We can all relate to our children wanting to just dive right in to the actual work, foregoing the preparation and clean-up stages that are an integral part of any project. The French culinary term of *mise en place* or

"putting in place" allows us to be ready to get to work safely and efficiently. On the other hand, clean-up is equally important.

- **Knowing when to follow:** You are not always the best leader. Know when to step down and take directions to get the problem solved.

25

Why do you need a coach or a mentor?

We, as individuals, think that we have our life together until we are hit by the realization of our life falling apart. You find yourself asking again and again, "Where did I go wrong?" Most of us fail to recognize the reasons. But it's never too late. You can always get a coach to help you out with the situations, specific or not. Here are the reasons why you need a coach or a mentor:

- To improve your leadership skills

  A coach analyses your inner thinking and as a result knows where your skill lies best. Most people are entrapped by their own mind to get what they want out of their lives. Life coaches help you in way that they will release your mind of all the toxic thoughts and actually take control of your life.

- To help you find direction

  Feeling lost can be frustrating especially if you are having a midlife crisis. Coaches help you to train your mind to get into a new framework that will help you to progress further. Also, they will make you understand that having a crisis does not necessarily mean that it's a bad thing.

- To help maintain focus

  It's very easy to lose focus once you have come to a certain stage. This can lead to frustration and paying attention to details that are neither important nor needed, causing you to stress out on trivial issues. Coaches have, as professionals, dealt with many such cases and know how to help you get back on track.

- Make you more responsible

    Coaches make you more responsible. Of course, it depends upon the cultural context in which you function but there are things universal that pushes you to retain balance in your life. A coach will help you see what you have in your hand, your resources and how to allocate them effectively to get the best results.

- To help you tackle challenges

    Sometimes, you might be the most rational person ever but being stuck in some situations might leave you confused and indecisive as to what to do. A coach will help you to become more capable of taking up new challenges. The more you challenge yourself, the more chances you have for healthy growth.

- Tackle problems in personal relationships

    Personal relationship conflicts may affect your other aspects of life. They may slow down your progress at work and other places. Even though we know it very well that personal and professional life should be kept apart, you might have a problem coping with it. If that is the case, a coach would be able to help you big time.

- Working towards your general wellbeing

  A coach can help you see many things in general. They push you to be a better person. They help you overcome your problems and anxieties. They help you do better, feel better and be a positive influence.

There you have it. The reason why you need a coach in your life. Do we need to be convinced more?

Smart networking for Leadership development

If you want to go fast, go alone; if you want to go far, go with others. The most successful people in the world, look for collaboration and build networks. Networking plays a pivotal role in leadership. Networking and building contacts are one of the boons that which leaders are blessed with. In a network there are people who you help and then there are also people who want to help you back. The best leaders are in fame today just because of their networking skills and contact. It's not who you know, but who knows you. Networking is just like marketing, marketing yourself, your uniqueness and what you stand for. Behind a successful you, there will be many successful relationships. Networking is more of an art but there are some basic guidelines that govern them.

- The "critical few" those are the people who matter. These are the top 20 in your contact list who matter the most to you; of course, professionally. Be very sure you are in constant touch and in good terms with them. These are the ones who matter most to your profession.

- Be a generous helping hand to anyone and everyone who genuinely needs assistance. This would not only earn you a grateful patron but also a worthy contact.
- Always make networks and contacts when you are not in need of them. This portrays a selfless picture in front of the person you are trying to be in touch with. People usually do not want someone hanging off their backs for favors, right in the first go.
- Try to be of help to the person you are trying to get into contact with. This will enhance your chances of connecting with him. If you are of some use to him, you are definitely going to land in their contact lists. If not, create a demand.
- One of the golden rules, in corporate networking is give before you ask. If you are of some assistance to them, offer them barter. This will have better chances of being a success.
- Think people, not positions. If you go for their position, they are going to block you off. Be subtle when you approach people and approach them on a personal level before getting down into business.
- Be genuine when it comes down to building relationships; always add a personal touch to any contact you land up with. This greatly enhances your credibility and your professional network as well.
- Know the people you are trying to connect with, research about them before approaching them. If you show interest towards them, they are likely to take interest in you.
- Be an avid listener and give valuable inputs. Be up to date with the affairs going on. Make the

audience feel that u notice and you care and that the audience matters to you.

Some of the various methods of networking include:

- Volunteering
- Social-media networking
- Event management and planning
- Corporate meetings and get-togethers
- Online networking

We can always pick what suits us best. Some of us are comfortable more with face to face networking compared to online networking. However with people getting busier nowadays the online networking flatforms are getting more popularity and we should be open to use them.

Personally I got benefited a lot with the linkedin platform. It's a wonderful tool for professional networking. In face I must tell you as an entrepreneur 50% of my business came from linkedin. All it takes is 15 to 20 minutes everyday.

Its indeed a wonderful platform where we can easily get connected with people who have similar passion and interest and eventually that network would get you a lot of like minded individuals to collaborate with you on your future initiatives.

So keep exploring new possibilities to network as networking is the mantra for successful leaders and Leaders are always in a lookout to create and use networks to get people, information and resources for accelerated growth.

As Leaders lets connect, collaborate and create.

26

Leading a happy and meaningful life

Putting down my tool sack, I hugged my wife as soon as I entered our little hut. The children were already asleep and the food was served. I quickly freshened up and sat down to eat.

"How was work today?"

"I have started working on another sculpture; the stone is porous and cracks even with the slightest of pressure. Glazing would take even longer. Being a stone mason is no joke these days, the art is almost extinct in this region. How was your day? I know these children would be a handful."

"Oh, never mind, I enjoy being around them when you go fend for us. I am really glad; we took the right decision to adopt and take them in. They are a bundle of joy."

"I wish I was better paid and had a better job to give you all a better life."

"I am so proud of you, you give us enough already, we have a roof, we have food in our tummy and can afford popsicles every Easter. You already give us a well-guarded life. "And with this, we finished our dinner and retired for the day.

No sooner did I hit the bed, then I started drowsing off. This was the best part of the day, to earn a good night's sleep after a day's worth of hard work. I was drifting away into oblivion when a bright light shown through the hole in the roof and I started walking towards it. It was a green valley and I went down a street to see the house of a merchant.

"Oh, how I wish I could be a merchant, to have so much of wealth and luxury."

As soon as he wished, he found himself as a merchant for a day. He was envied and hated by people who were less wealthy than him. At night, he was unable to sleep thinking of safeguarding all that money stashed in his safe.

Just then, I saw a high official in a Limousine, who was revered and bowed down by all. He went ahead with a procession of security vans. "Well, how wealthy and powerful he might be. I wish I could be that!" and again his wish was granted. He was seated in the Limousine but the AC of the Limousine was not working as the sun shone so bright on the roof. He was irked by this and thought, "How I wish I could be the sun, the most powerful" and then he became the sun, shining bright and scorching over the entire world.

Soon after that he was overshadowed by the clouds and again, he wished if he could be the cloud. And his wish was granted again. He became a mighty roaring black cloud overshadowing the sun and raining havoc over land, when he was blown away by the wind, releasing all his moisture.

"I guess the wind is more powerful, I should be the wind!" and he was turned into a gust of strong wind, blowing away all the trees leaves and the roof tops of houses, but then he realized, he could not move the rocks.

"The rocks are more powerful then. I want to be a huge rock, strong and unmovable. And then he became a rock, more powerful than anything else I the earth. But as he has seated there, unmoving, he could feel the pounding of a hammer and chisel, into his hard exterior. He felt as if his shape and size were changing.

"What could possibly be more powerful than I, the rock?" he thought to himself.

He glanced down far below him, to see the figure of a stone mason with his tools, chiseling his way into the rock.

I woke up alarmed and startled and saw it was already 5 AM. That day, when I saw my reflection in the mirror, I thought of the dream I had seen. I was happy, content and powerful in my own way.

We often run after money, power and luxury and almost forget to appreciate what we have in our present which fends for us and caters after us to make ends meet. It is the law of nature says that nature can provide for our needs but not for our greed. Similarly, aiming for what is enough and sufficient for the body and soul is what should be looked after.

Self-contentment and satisfaction with the resources that are available to us ensures for a happy life that is striving for more; not lusting for more. Not only self-contentment ensures peace of mind, but also ensures a peaceful life. One of our greatest tests is to see if we are able to bless someone while going through our own adversity.

Helping others will only add to the network of friends and acquaintances which will lead to a happy social life. Being a social animal, one should always try to have a good camaraderie among his neighbors. Only by giving are you able to receive more than you already have. Helping one person might not change the whole world, but it could change the world for one person. We can't help everyone, but everyone can help someone.

Love is what binds people together; even simple gestures of love and affection can greatly motivate and ensure a person of their worth and ability. Love has the power of sealing even the roughest and deepest of cracks. It is found that, if you love life, life loves you back. Every soul in this world, wants appreciation and acceptance and the best way to convey it is through love.

Passion is the driving force that makes your work place an adventurous journey. A great leader's courage to fulfil his vision comes from his passion, not from his position. Allow your passion to become your purpose and soon after watch it converts into your profession.

Diligence is the secret to a happy and content life. Hard work pays off eventually. What we hope to do with ease and fluent must first be practiced with diligence and passion.

The definition of leading a happy and a meaningful life is different for different people. But love, Passion, Diligence, contentment and helping others are some of the common factors that make sure you lead a meaningful life.

At times we are so taken and engrossed in our professional lives that we forget there is a life outside our laptops and our offices.

Once the CEO of a well-known company was lounging on a beach of Mexico. While relaxing, he noticed a fisherman unloading his catch. Out of curiosity the CEO asked,

"How long did it take to catch them?"

"Not long!" replied the fisherman.

"You should have stayed longer in the seas that would have been a terrific catch." Opined the CEO.

"But sir, this is enough for me and my family."

"What will you do with the rest of your time?"

"I take 8 hours' worth of sleep and toil in the waters for a good day's catch. I spend time with my family. Play and teach my children. Spend time with my wife and help her cook and wash. In the evening I make my children learn skills and teach and train them. And on some evenings, I meet up my friends, have drinks, sing and make merry by playing music. My life is full."

The surprised CEO replied. "I can help you figure this out better. I am an MBA from a well-recognized university. You should spend all time possible in the waters. Keep fishing till you are exhausted. Sell the extra fish and earn profits."

"What happens after that?"

"Well you buy a new boat. With that you fish more, eventually get a fleet and hire staffs. With all the profits, you can directly sell to the processing units and set up your own company."

"And then?"

"You can sell the shares of the company and earn in millions."

"How long will all of this take?" "A couple of decades at max." "What happens after that?"

"Well this is the fun part. You can retire on this very coast. Spend time on your bed, enjoy siestas....do a little bit of fishing here and there, play with your grandchildren, hangout with your old buddies, drink and make merry for the remainder of your life."

Hearing this, the fisherman smiled a desolate smile, shrugged his shoulders and walked away leaving a perplexed, CEO.

The fisherman was whispering – why wait for 20 years if I am experiencing the same fun now.

So, you need to decide whether you want to be happy now or wait for happiness to come at a time when you will not have a lot of energy and enthusiasm to enjoy those happy moments.

So, keep doing the following:

- Play according to your strengths and spend time and energy only to those areas where you excel or want to excel.
- Learn to keep work hours work for you. Try to finish off work within the stipulated work hours. Remember you have a solid 8 hours in a day dedicated to work, so you can do a lot in 8 hours.
- Prioritize your tasks. Prioritizing is a method of letting know what matters more and what matters less. Choose wisely.
- Take time to make time. It is not always possible to find time out of a busy schedule but make sure you let your mind and body rejuvenate by giving yourself at least ten minutes every day.
- Find time for exercise. It is a must do, not a should do. Exercise keeps your mind and body active.
- Motivate and be motivated, it is food for a rejuvenated life.

- Take time to read every day, it is solace for a tired mind, and food for thought.
- Let your people, both at home and work know that you are there for them. These little gestures go a long way. Lot of people even refer to the team at work as their work family.
- Make time to do what you love. This will keep you sane, satiated and composed with yourself, at least you will be sure that you did justice to yourself.
- Take a break from work at frequent intervals. Go for a holiday that your body and mind need. If you have a country or a place in your mind, please do some research about the people and the unique things in the place before you visit. It would change your holidays to those perfect holidays which would be memorable forever.
- Most importantly keep asking these questions to you frequently and act.

    1. Do you have the freedom to be you ? Remember it should be mostly what you want to do and not what others want you to do in life.

    2. Do you have a Mental picture of where you would like to be ?

    3. Are you Thinking Less and Doing More ? As we are in an information age, there are so many things around you and it leads you to think so much. However the idea is not to be caught by the bug of overthinking and start doing things more and more.

    4. Are you doing what you say and saying what you do ? if you are not practicing this your mind will constantly giving you inputs that you

Are We Leading?

    are not doing much for yourself and that will bring down your confidence levels and your growth. Also by repeatedly saying what you will do you are reaffirming yourself that you will consistently act.

5. Are you consistently learning something new to lead consistently ?

6. Are you getting consumed ? Do you have any energy left to lead ? we are in a transactional world where so much is expected from us and even if we don't want to give importance somehow we get dragged. But if too much of that is happening you would not be able to give much time to what you want to focus in your life.

7. Are you in a position to accept things around you ? Total Acceptance is accepting You the way you are and offcourse – accepting things around you they way they are.

8. Do you have gratitude for yourself, your Environment, People around you and for the bright future you want to experience. If Yes do you express it everyday ?

27

Closure: It's all about a leadership mindset

Have you ever wanted something so bad but did not get it? Do you ever wonder if you could have done something differently and achieved what you wanted? Do you wish you could have gotten second chances?

I will let you know a secret. You can! How? The answer is simple and yet so complex. It's by changing and regulating your mindset.

Before I tell you about how to go about it, let us define it for you so that there is no confusion regarding what it is.

"A mindset is a belief that orients the way we handle situations — the way we sort out what is going on and what we should do. Our mindset helps us spot opportunities but they can trap us in self-defeating cycles." (Psychology today)

Re-read the definition that we have stated above. You would notice that it has a positive as well as a negative thought attached to it. On one hand it can help you to spot opportunities on the other it can trap you in self-defeating cycles.. Once you make your mindset the strength, nothing will stop you from achieving what you want.

So, the million-dollar question here (literally, if you want it) is how to change your mindset in such a way that you achieve what you want?

Here are a few examples of mindsets that we tend to develop over time.

- Fixed vs. growth mindset

    Fixed mindset makes people stagnant because people who have fixed mindset do not take responsibility of their mistakes. This stops the brain from taking any responsibility for improvement. People with growth mindset however; tend to work on growth by learning from their mistakes of the past.

- Preoccupied vs. eager

    People who have preoccupied thoughts tend to leave little breathing space for new ideas to grow in their head. People who are eager are quite the questioning type which also let them to find the answers to it. You can decide for yourself which one is more productive.

- Wanting to build trust vs. cold and detached

    Some people just value relations/understand the reason they need to build and keep them. Such people put more effort into building long lasting trusting relations. This also allows them vulnerability and emotional openness. People that come off as cold and detached are much more emotionally fragile, have difficulty expressing emotions and tend to be more stuck up on things than the usual.

- Relying on cooperation vs. relying on compliance
    People who tend to believe in goodwill trust others to cooperate with them, mostly with positive results. People who believe in making people comply with them tend to be more ruthless and

unpopular. People of the former category know that it takes time to build trust and they work on it. People who believe that compliance is the answer, tend to view everyone with suspicion.

- Pattern followers vs. problem solvers

People who show consistent growth are usually the ones that are problem solvers. They take up new challenges and tend to put their creativity to solve new problems. People who follow patterns lack the ability to question and challenge and in general fail to deal with problems.

These are the most common mindset types people fall into. They could have combinations of them in any extent. It depends on their nature about how to act and react to certain situations. This sets the field for further mindset shift or development. Here is where the good news lies.

And the good news is mindsets can be changed with a little effort. Although it will take some work, it'll pay off in the end. The effects would also be relatively long term. Here are a few things to practice if you want to create a shift in your mindset.

- Acknowledge that you are different and put it to the best use. Everyone is built differently. They have their own experiences and approaches. They work according to that. Recognize your own assets (you can ask a trusted guardian to do it for you as well). Your strengths and improvement areas define you. Don't stop yourself from achieving anything on the basis of your weaknesses.

- Motivate yourself

  People say motivation does not work. However, I have always experienced that it gives you that initial kick to start something. However, in a long run we need to attach some kind of feeling and emotions with our goals. The simple visualization of what all you can experience once you achieve your goals can be a wonderful and can consistently motivate you.

- Learn the ability to appreciate.

  This goes a long way- kind words, good intentions and genuine appreciation. Apply these in your life. These create a very positive environment. This will help you be in a positive mood, elevating your work environment and the people around you. Remember people love to be rewarded and recognized.

- Take up one idea.

  Take up one idea. Make that one idea your life- think of it, dream of it, live on that idea. Let the brain, heart, muscles, nerves, every part of your body be full of that idea. That is the way to lead yourself to success. This is what Swamy Vivekananda believed and followed all his life.

- Search, Research and learn

  They say – **we don't know what we don't know**. So, there is a need to search and research. Take your time to figure out stuff. Read some self-help books. Try different adventures and learn about different cultures. Explore how both western and eastern philosophies to lead life can be a great combination for accelerated growth.

Before I end this chapter I would like to share my recommended list of things which you can practice to create a Leadership mindset which will lead to happiness and success.

Mindfulness – which is based on Indian and eastern meditation practices. It is a directed focus style of meditation where you are directing your focus on some thing. Everyone advices you live in present and not to worry about your past or future but the moment you ask them how to be in present they say you need to figure out yourself. Mindfulness techniques are an answer to it. It **is a wonderful technique to keep you in the present moment so that you can utilize the power of now.**

NLP: If you still don't know about NLP its not a big deal. However what is surprising is NLP which is so proven and powerful for self transformation has not yet reached to many of us. By the way I am talking about Neuro Linguistic programming and not Natural language processing (something which is related to artificial intelligence stuff)

My sincere suggestion to all of you would be to start reading about NLP (Neuro Linguistic programming). I have personally gained a lot and I am sure all of us will have a similar experience.

NLP has been around since 1970's and has been a huge success so far in changing lives.

Neuro refers to our nervous system, which links our five senses by which we see, hear, feel, smell and taste. Linguistic refers to our language - how we speak, what we speak, our body language and emotions. Programming is how we program our thoughts, feelings, actions or habits in a way that it helps us achieve what we want.

NLP techniques help you to be more effective at personal and professional levels.You would be able to develop desired patterns and modify your behavior rapidly. Especially it would help you a great deal if you currently need an immediate resolution to an existing problem or a set of problems – something which has been bothering you a lot and you are dying to get over it.

So either you can search for happiness in your whole life or just experience happiness now. The choice is yours

Ikigai : Ikigai is a Japanese concept which means 'reason for being'.

Everyone has one, but finding it can take effort and the effort is worth for leading your life.

Ten rules – To find your own ikigai :

- Stay active
- Leave urgency behind and adopt a slower pace of life
- Contribute at work
- Surround yourself with good friends at work
- Get in shape through daily, gentle exercise
- Smile and acknowledge people in your team
- Reconnect with nature
- Gratitude for anything that brightens your day.
- Live in the moment
- Follow your ikigai

Hygge : Hygge, pronounced "hoo-guh", is a gift from the most happiest country Denmark to the whole world. Hygge means - taking pleasure in ordinary moments to achieve contentment in life.

It means creating an environment to celebrate life within yourself and family and friends.

It's about relaxing everyday and showing gratitude to everything which you have in life

Its about Celebrating ordinary moments like they're extraordinary.

Ontological Approach to Leadership Development:

An ontological approach is all about asking yourself - who are we ? what are we here for ? whats the purpose ?

Leadership is a combination of the Leader's language and action and its our Language, emotions and our body create our world.

I would recommend you to further research on these topics and start learning more from experts.

Just to conclude – Developing a new mindset will take a little time. Be consistent with it. It will require patience. It is also a good idea to understand the reason why you have developed a certain mindset. This will help you understand the root cause of a mindset that you deem to be harmful to you.

Do not be disheartened if you have temporary setbacks. Remember, you want to be successful and successful people never stop trying.

Stop waiting. It is time to act.

Are We Leading?

People say work hard, believe in yourself. In fact, there are a plethora of self-help books in the market. However, are they enough? The best thing is to get some personal guidance and some tips from people who actually are practicing it day in and out.

Bruce Lee once said - Defeat is not defeat unless accepted as a reality in your own mind.

You are here because you have decided to be here. **Everyone makes the best choices available to them at the time they make them.** so, there is nothing we should regret.

In our human mind there is always a juggle between negative and positive feelings. These feelings are all based on what is being fed to our mind. If you start feeding more positive information and feedback, then you will automatically feel positive and act positive.

When you are positive, people just get attracted to you and your vision. you quickly build relationships which helps you to lead. Remember no leader is successful on their own.

So ultimately your positive attitude and mindset is your power and it would always enable you to lead your life in all aspects.

Keep Leading and 'Life would never be the same again'.

Frequently Asked Questions

My answers to some of the frequently asked questions in terms of Leadership and leading the life you want.

Q) How do you define leadership?

A) Leadership is a commitment to achieve something new and something which is unrealistic to other people. It's about continuously improving yourself and people around you.

The definition of leadership has nothing to do with the hierarchy or anyone's position.

Q) Is leadership only for Corporate or Business or Politics or for all?

A) Well anyone can be a leader. we can lead as an individual, as an employee, as a parent as a child as a responsible citizen.

The Job of leaders is not taking power, but the opposite: Empowering.

Q) Are Leaders born or made?

A) I know It's a never-ending debate. I would say Both- but mostly made.

Some people are born with qualities that make them natural leaders, and other people acquire it by training, practice and experience. They seek to understand and be understood.

However irrespective of whether they are born or made they should continuously improve their ability with desire, determination and focus.

Q) Is Leadership all about motivation?

A) Motivational leadership refers to someone leading others by motivating them. It definitely gives you that initial push. The beginning to everything is the hardest part. Motivation also help you to appreciate the situation and Look at the brighter side.

However, Motivation is always short lived.

Q) Can you suggest few tools and techniques in order to get started in terms of leading a happy and successful life.

A) A combination of Meditation and NLP (Neuro Linguistic programming) has tremendously worked for me.

Human beings have huge potential to grow beyond our current limitations. However, we get limited by our own beliefs, our own thoughts and our own values, our own feelings, our own opinions and our own judgement. we keep holding to them and it does not allow us to move forward.

Meditation and NLP helps you to get rid of these limitations. Meditation mainly works on self-awareness as a Leader and NLP helps you to train your brain and achieving excellence in both your personal and professional life.

Both these tools help you to stay in a happy and beautiful state of mind no matter what people do to you. Happy people are successful

Q) How do we define the quality of life

A) How well you lead your life is directly proportional to how much you love yourself and others. The heart is much more wiser than your head. Trust your instincts and follow it.

Q) I feel I am being consumed every day. where do I take out energy to lead?

A) In this transactional life, you would always be consumed with things - others want you to do. However, you need to give equal importance to what you want to do. Wherever focus goes energy flows.

Also, If you don't use the energy, you lose it. Silent and passive people don't learn much and hence can't lead effectively.

Q) Your three favorite quotes on Leadership.

A) 1) There is an extraordinary in every ordinary.

2) Everyone has a success story however only a few people realize it.

3) The best investment in Leading is the investment in Learning.

These are quotes which I wrote for myself sometime back and has influenced me a lot so far.

Q) Does affirmations help in Leading life effectively ? what are your favorite ones.

A) Affirmations always keep you on track. Some of my favorite ones which helps me to lead my life are:

Affirmation 1: I would be in a beautiful state always, appreciate things around me and empower myself to lead.

Affirmation 2: No matter what the situation is - I would find out a way.

Affirmation 3: I would always push myself hard to achieve more.

Are We Leading?

Q) How can I Train myself on Leadership?

A) You can attend Leadership Training and Coaching workshops where you get exposed to leadership models and a tailored approach to create a positive ecosystem for yourself so that you can contribute to the best of your potential.

Indian Leadership Academy provides such Leadership Development programs to create self motivated individuals who have a vision to lead from the front, have strong passion and attitude to lead themselves as well as others. The Programs help you to assess your style of leadership and provide opportunities to identify specific areas of improvement and ultimately lead the life you deserve.

Visit us at : www.indianleadershipacademy.com

Indian Leadership Academy - Workshops

Indian Leaders - Global Audience

www.ingramcontent.com/pod-product-compliance
Lightning Source LLC
Chambersburg PA
CBHW020913180526
45163CB00007B/2714